The War Stole My Soul with Post-Traumatic Stress Disorder (PTSD): What Now?

The War Stole My Soul with Post-Traumatic Stress Disorder (PTSD): What Now?

C. Diane Mosby

Foreword by
Katie G. Cannon

RESOURCE *Publications* · Eugene, Oregon

THE WAR STOLE MY SOUL WITH POST-TRAUMATIC
STRESS DISORDER (PTSD): WHAT NOW?

Resource Publications
An Imprint of Wipf and Stock Publishers
199 W. 8th Ave., Suite 3
Eugene, OR 97401

www.wipfandstock.com

PAPERBACK ISBN: 978-1-5326-3861-9
HARDCOVER ISBN: 978-1-5326-3862-6
EBOOK ISBN: 978-1-5326-3863-3

Manufactured in the U.S.A.

These pages are dedicated to the brave men and women of the United States Armed Forces who serve this country with dignity and courage. Your great sacrifice in the face of dangers, seen and unseen, has made living in this country better for many who often forget to say, *"Thank You."*

This project is for those who may not be aware of all you give. This project was done to raise awareness to those who engage these pages, of the sacrifices you make, and the ultimate price you pay emotionally, physically, mentally, and spiritually so that we, the citizens of these United States of America, may continue to enjoy our freedom.

To my son, Geoffrey Andre' Mosby, Jr., veteran of Operation Iraqi Freedom (OIF).

Thank you for your bravery in the midst of suffering and for teaching all of us what real courage looks like in the face of the greatest *war* of your life, Post-Traumatic Stress Disorder (PTSD).

Without your story, this project would never be.

Contents

List of Tables

Foreword

I AM GLAD DR. C. Diane Mosby wrote *The War Stole My Soul with Post-Traumatic Stress Disorder (PTSD): What Now?* and I will keep it handy. Her words provide 'a balm in Gilead' for my fifty-year old, soul-injured wounds. Balm in Gilead, a spiritual hymn based on a verse in the Old Testament, Jeremiah 8:22, refers to holy, sacred, divine medicine that is able "to make the wounded whole... to heal the sin-sick soul."

In 1967, when I entered college, the coeds gathered in the basement of Faith Hall for mail call, a time filled with angst, anger, and fear. Replicated time and time again, with routine occurrences, we heard chilling, shrieking screams of grief when friends received news about the death of love ones, kith and kin, fathers, brothers, sisters, spouses, fiancés, and friends who faced the ultimate test of patriotism, and now they were being shipped home in body bags, placed in caskets that could never be opened.

As African American students matriculating at historically Black colleges (HBCUs), we were aware of the disproportionate number of African Americans drafted and sent to the front lines in Vietnam. We discussed how hawks-of-war, the official stakeholders, demanded African American military personnel to acquiesce without complaint, desist from protest, accommodate whiteness, conform in tangible ways to outmoded vestiges of separate but unequal Jim Crowism, all in all, the manifestation of systemic alienation of Black people from our God-given human being-ness.

Oftentimes, we talked throughout the night, analyzing and strategizing about disastrous inequities faced both on the battlefield

FOREWORD

and here at home. Members of our churches and hometown communities were overseas fighting a war in Vietnam, while others of us, who were stateside, fought a never-ending battle against the insidious acts of violence perpetrated by dominant powerbrokers who worked in collusion with terrorist vigilantes, such as the Ku Klux Klan.

A significant number of coeds, returning from combat, used military and veteran scholarships to enroll in college. In the 1960s, given the sensitive conditions of student-soldiers, we referred to their fitful, erratic behavior as being "shell-shocked," a phrased coined in World War I. However, during our candlelight vigils, wherein we protested war and marched around the campus quadrangle for peace, several veterans manifested symptoms of not being able to talk, walk, nor act rationally. Our classmates' physical and emotional inabilities are no longer referred to as being "shell-shocked." We now know the contemporary expression for our comrades' wartime afflictions is post-traumatic stress disorder (PTSD).

This book, *The War Stole My Soul with Post-Traumatic Stress Disorder (PTSD): What Now?* by Dr. Mosby, is a welcoming illumination of the fragments and fissures in the lives of military veterans and family members regarding traumas of fight-or-flight. Due to lack of sufficient knowledge and proficiency, far too often, clergy and laity, family members and friends, dismiss, minimize, or stand paralyzed during and after a loved one experiences flashbacks of the intense horrors they have encountered.

Moreover, according to Dr. Mosby, the majority of women and men "commissioned by God to provide soul care," such as denominational executives, ordained pastors, and installed church officers, are unable to serve as credible, trusted, reliable support in the healing process. In turn, when men and women of the United States Armed Forces seek our assistance in juxtaposing their battle fatigue and combat stress in relations to God's grace and mercy, we must be able and willing to address the challenges of PTSD. Death by suicide among veterans is excessively high. Many of us have never been soldiers in combat, but yet throughout our lives

xii

we have witnessed, up close and personal, the causalities of warfare. Mosby, writing in a clear and inviting style, offers forgiveness, healing, and restoration to each of us.

I thank Dr. Mosby for *The War Stole My Soul with Post-Traumatic Stress Disorder (PTSD): What Now?* This book is a foundational text for those of us called and committed to the kinetic mining of our ministerial awareness, ability, and aptitude in relations to post-traumatic stress disorder. With studious tenacity and forceful integrity, Mosby offers training, information, and resources pertinent to caring for the souls of veterans within our faith communities, men and women who fought in wars in which the USA was involved since 1945—soldiers on battlefields in places such as Europe, Japan, Korea, Viet Nam, Iran, Iraq, Desert Storm, Afghanistan—as well as the women and men returning home daily from military service.

The Reverend Katie G. Cannon, PhD
Annie Scales Rogers Professor of Christian Social Ethics
Union Presbyterian Seminary in Richmond, VA

Preface

AS MANY VETERANS RETURN to United States from the wars of Iraq and Afghanistan, they struggle with one of its remnants, known as Post-Traumatic Stress Disorder (PTSD). PTSD, an anxiety disorder resulting from exposure to trauma, leaves its sufferers struggling to find assistance with healing and restoration. Statistics reveal that 40 percent of veterans will seek their clergy as a trusted resource in the healing process.

As stated by Reverend Edgar W. Hatcher, retired chaplain, U.S. Air Force:

The truth is that war permanently changes the people who fight it. It produces tremendous moral and spiritual residue which impacts the veterans and their families. The church is a powerful force in helping veterans wrestle with and reconcile the love of God with the horrors they encounter and protect us from. Most pastors are woefully unprepared for ministry in these circumstances.[1]

The local pastor, commissioned by God to provide *soul care* to the suffering, is the context for this project. This *soul care*, which provides assistance with core beliefs, reconciliation with God, and renewed relationships with church and community, can be achieved only when pastors and clergy are made more aware of the challenges of those in their congregations and communities, and when they are given the tools and resources to address those needs with training, information, and referral.

1. Edgar W. Hatcher, "Care for Returning Veterans Workshop," Lutheran Theological Southern Seminary // News, September 10, 2008, accessed October 23, 2010, http://www.ltss.edu/news/latest-news/32/.

To address this growing concern and the missing resource on the issue of PTSD from not only a psychological and clinical perspective, but also as a soul care concern, it was necessary to collaborate with another source and equip another population of interveners—the pastor. For this project thirteen local pastors were educated and trained on PTSD.

The training provided education on the symptoms, noted struggles, and issues of *soul care* of those who suffer with this ailment. The results of Pre-Test and Post-Test instruments, as well as a Post-Training questionnaire, affirm that the training was effective in increasing the participants' knowledge of PTSD and subsequently motivated them to address PTSD in their respective congregations.

Acknowledgments

I WISH TO THANK my faithful editor, Dr. Harold E. Pinkston, Sr., for his unfailing support and honest feedback, and for continuing to hold me to "The Standard." God sent you to me, and I am humbled. To my advisor, Dr. Nathaniel West, who would not allow me to settle, but pressed me for excellence. You are appreciated more than you know. Dr. Katie G. Canon—your review of this work, your scholarly advice, and support of my efforts are held dear to my heart. Thank you for being such a blessing to my life. You have touched me immensely.

Dr. John W. Kinney and the faculty and staff of the Samuel Dewitt Proctor School of Theology at Virginia Union University— words cannot express my deep gratitude for all you have imparted into my life. Your faith in me challenged me to see more in myself and to pursue greater heights. I am eternally grateful.

Many thanks to my contextual associates and project observers: Reverend Dr. Sabrina St. Clair, Mrs. Carol Watkins, Mrs. Lisa Overton, Reverend Lamont Gooding, Dr. Stephen Hewlett, and Reverend Cholon Coleman, who read and reread this document and provided great insight and honest critique; thank you for being my midwives and not allowing me to abort in midterm.

To my friend and colleague, Reverend Angelo V. Chatmon: I know God placed you in my life for such a time as this. You never let me give up, give out, or give away this dream. Thank you for your obedience to God to see me through this season in my life. I am forever grateful.

ACKNOWLEDGMENTS

To Dr. Walter Parrish, Executive Director of American Baptist Churches of the South (ABCOTS); Dr. Stephen Hewlett, Moderator of the Shiloh Baptist Association; Dr. Robert Pettis, Moderator of the Tuckahoe Baptist Association; Dr. Patricia Gould-Champ, Pastor of the Faith Community Baptist Church; Dr. Mark White, Pastor of the Chamberlayne Baptist Church; the Clarksville, Tennessee Society of Human Resource Management (SHRM); and Foster Meadors of the Veteran Mobile Center: you have my greatest appreciation for allowing me to pilot this project with your churches and organizations. Your support and belief in this work are reflected in its outcome.

Anointed New Life Baptist Church, what a privilege I have to provide vision and to serve with the greatest servants of God. Thank you for allowing me to be what God would have me to be. Your support, sacrifice, prayers, and love kept me lifted in some lonely, dark places. God knew who I would need during this process, and I am grateful it was you.

To all my family who sacrificed my presence at family gatherings for three years, thanks for understanding, praying, and supporting.

To my children: Tara, Teresa, Alloysius, Andre', Donnitria; and to my grandchildren: Jalik, Camille, Naomi, Alaya, Isaiah, Jeremiah, Kaden, Zion, and Tre'; to my brothers and sisters: Wayne, Jesse, David, Teresa, Monique, Sharon; and to my mother, Joyce Streater—if I had a thousand tongues it would not be enough to express my love and gratitude for you. You understand the meaning of sacrifice better than anyone I know. Thanks for allowing me to pursue this dream so that we all can be witness of God's glory. To Edward D. Greene, Jr. and Mrs. Roberta B. Claiborne (my Ganny)—gone but never forgotten.

Finally, to my husband, Geoffrey, for the dreams we dreamed, the victories we have seen, the storms we have endured, and the expectation of the joys to come. You are the *Man's* man, and I love you!

Introduction

THE GLOBAL WAR ON Terrorism has been a devastating reality to the United States of America and to the culture of the American people. Though the wars of Operation Enduring Freedom (OEF) and Operation Iraqi Freedom (OIF) have been fought on the foreign soils of Afghanistan and Iraq, the impact to the American people cannot be ignored.

Whether we care to acknowledge it or not, we have become conscious of the wars' impact on our culture each time we travel. In American airports, we are now bombarded with security measures dictated by the Department of Homeland Security and the Transportation Safety Administration (TSA). Travelers are screened through airport security. One's body is scanned by wand or x-ray. Carry-on luggage is x-rayed or searched to ensure that only acceptable items will enter the aircraft. All of this is done as a proactive measure to eliminate explosives or other dangerous weapons, to calm the fears of the American public, and to secure safety.

Another impact of war that has made its way to American soil is the staggering number of veterans from OEF and OIF who are suffering with the invisible wounds of war, such as the wounds we identify as Post-Traumatic Stress Disorder (PTSD). Recent statistics released by the Department of Veterans Affairs report approximately 300,000 veterans of the Iraq and Afghanistan wars—nearly 20 percent of the returning forces—are likely to suffer from either PTSD or other major depressions. These numbers are likely to climb.

The reality of these impacts found their way to my doorstep and into the tapestry of our family life in February 2005. It was my son's return from a tour of combat duty in Mosul, Iraq that brought the wars and their effects back to Glen Allen, Virginia. His journey with PTSD altered my world and the world of those around us, as we watched our loved one spiral into the abyss of darkness that, seemingly, no light could penetrate.

Our attempts to find assistance through the United States Department of Veterans Affairs (VA), the Virginia Department of Veterans Services, and the McGuire Veterans Affairs Medical Center were frantic and futile. My disappointment and frustration with the required documentation processes that veterans had to endure, coupled with the lack of counselors available for intervention, and the disparity in compensation decisions, pushed me to action.

Initially, I began a personal quest to learn all I could about the disorder, and what concerned family members could do to assist their loved ones to get the medical and financial assistance they needed. It was during this process of exploration that another emerging population of interveners kept coming to the forefront as a potential resource for help. This population was the local pastor.

In my research, a recurring statistic kept appearing. That statistic stated that four out of every ten sufferers would seek out their clergy for help before they would go to the VA hospital or to a professional psychologist or counselor for help. They saw the clergy as a known and safe resource.

This information, coupled with my passion to bring more attention to the plight and needs of our veterans and their families, drew my attention to the need for pastors and clergy to become educated and aware of this growing issue. The need for this project and the focus and impetus of this manuscript were born from this reality.

The work which engages this document is entitled, "When the War Comes Home with Post-Traumatic Stress Disorder (PTSD): Now What? What Pastoral Leaders Need to Know." This study identifies the void of conversation and the lack of awareness of the plight of those with PTSD among pastors who serve local congregations. This study also identifies the clergy's need to be educated and made aware of the symptoms, facts, challenges, and needs of those who are a part of the congregations they serve.

It is my contention that psychologists, counselors, and clinicians may address behavioral symptoms and needs related to the illness, but there is a void in the spiritual wellness of the patient that has not been addressed. The struggles many sufferers have with issues of spirituality are not being addressed. This is a *soul care* issue for many who are looking for a reconnection with their core beliefs and God. Pastors are called to this work and, thus, need to be aware of a growing population and demographic that will be seeking their help in the healing process.

This document is the result of this study.

Chapter 1 discusses my approach and style of ministry and covers my ministry context. The problem and its perspectives, preliminary research, and results from a pilot presentation can be found in this chapter.

Chapter 2 presents my literature review. During my review of the available literature, I discovered that there was little to no dialogue or consideration as to how the local pastor or clergy may be a resource in the facilitation of restoration and healing. Nor was there much reference that addressed the need for pastoral education or training about PTSD.

Chapter 3 offers a theoretical foundation for the model. It is my intention to raise the Biblical paradigm as recorded in Chapter 37 of Ezekiel, known as the valley of dry bones. I contend that the agents of God (pastors) must first believe that change to dead, dry bones is possible with the intervention of God. The pastor's or clergy's belief and willingness to be an agent for God is critical to the restoration of those who are suffering and have lost hope. That same principle applies to the role of the pastor as the agent of God to those with PTSD.

Chapter 4 outlines the treatment relative to the problem. The treatment I offer for the lack of education and awareness is a series of training sessions on the subject for pastors who serve local congregations. The model design includes the following subject matter:

- What is PTSD?
- Facts about PTSD
- Symptoms of PTSD
- The Military in our Midst (video clip by PBS/Frontline 20/20)
- Challenges in Returning Home
- Spiritual Symptoms
- Spiritual Symptoms of Combat Trauma
- Why the Need for Pastors and Clergy?
- Pastors and Community Response

The assessments include a Pre-test and a Post-test, a Participants form, and Post-training interviews of selected participants.

Chapter 5 records the execution of the process, including the preliminary preparation, the execution of the treatment (workshop), and the observer's documentation of the proceedings.

In closing, Chapter 6 discusses the project evaluation, including demographic data, the analysis and the results of the Pre-test and Post-test, the results of the Post-training interviews, and my findings and summary.

It is my hope that the reader engaging this document will become sensitized to the materials, will become more aware of the plight and needs of our veterans and their family members, and will be enlightened by the content of the urgency for pastoral education, awareness, as well as the sufferer's need for *soul care*.

Chapter 1

Ministry Focus

Approach and Style of Ministry

WHILE GROWING UP IN rural Hanover County, I witnessed my great-grandmother serve as a deaconess, my grandmother provide care for the sick and shut-in of the community, and my mother open her home as a safe place to the neighborhood children. I am nourished by these examples of caring and nurturing that were etched in my early psyche.

I am fully aware that if I am to serve God, I must serve Him faithfully. It is clear to me that one's roots for service grow out of one's relationship with God, one's training in the church, and one's response to the needs of people. The women in my life were examples of hard work, service, giving, compassion, and faith. Not only did they believe the Word of God, but they also lived it in service to others. These models taught me that ministry is a sincere effort and commitment to take care of one's community with love, service, justice, faith, and an unshakeable trust in God. These were the only models for ministry that I knew at the time.

With that undergirding, I found myself in early adulthood seeking ministry in a context that I knew, and one with which I was familiar, namely, the local church. It was in the local church that I found my impetus. It was in the local church that I sought ways to be of service to the community. I desired to bring the community (as much as possible) into the church.

God revealed voids and the missing voices in the context of holistic ministry. He pressed me to address those needs. As Samuel Proctor states in My Moral Odyssey, "The Kingdom of God is more than an ethereal desire or wish; it presses toward practical expression."[1]

My practical expression found itself in the development of several ministries that were birthed in the context of the local church, but, to a larger extent, that expression served the expanding community. Through experiences in my ministerial odyssey, I have discovered that by keeping my ear in tune with the people in the community and my heart open to the needs of the community, I will be in a more productive mode to cultivate the art of community outreach and services. It is my passion to help the faith-based community of the church to see the greater needs of the people inside and outside the local church. It is my burning desire to serve the greater community which has directly and indirectly informed my spiritual and ministerial journey.

Context for Ministry

I have pursued two vocations most of my adult life. For twenty-three years, I worked for the Commonwealth of Virginia while serving in the local church. In 2004, God made it very clear that He wanted me to give my full attention to the local church. After seeking God's direction, I left my career as Business Manager for the Virginia Department of Transportation (VDOT) in 2005, and began my work in full-time ministry at a local church.

Business Administrator was my first assignment with the church. This position afforded me the opportunity to experience the dynamics of the day-to-day operational needs of the church. That assignment quickly evolved into my next appointment as Executive Minister.

1. Samuel Proctor, *Samuel Proctor: My Moral Odyssey* (Judson Press: Valley Forge), 1989, 110.

It was during this transition that God broadened my view of the role of the church being the impetus. He heightened my desire to be the positive impact of change in the community. He expanded my understanding of the needs of the community, and showed me, in a deeper sense, issues of the soul.

Providing spiritual care through the bereavement ministry of the local church brought me face-to-face with all three. As I walked with families through their loss, through their issues of grief, depression, isolation, disbelief, and anger toward God, my sensitivities were heightened. The trauma of losing a loved one and the emotional stages of grief sensitized me to the needs of another population of persons within our congregation and community, namely, those suffering with PTSD (Post-Traumatic Stress Disorder). During this same period of time, my son was diagnosed with symptoms of PTSD. As I witnessed my son's withdrawal from family, friends, society, and God, I began to live firsthand the issues of spiritual distress. During this time, God was preparing me for another work. Not long after I accepted the responsibility to serve as Executive Minister, God proceeded to "trouble the waters" of my life once again. He made it clarion clear through my grappling, restlessness, and emptiness that He was about to move me to yet another assignment.

In November 2008, the call became unquestionably distinct, and I answered His call to plant a church in the Richmond, Virginia area. In January 2009, I obediently responded to His call. God showed me, again, why I had to respond to His call with obedience. A further period of preparation was not only ushering me into my next assignment in ministry, but it was also preparing me for my next assignment in ministry as an advocate for our armed service members and veterans.

In April 2009, the *Anointed New Life Baptist Church (ANLBC)* was birthed for the Kingdom of God. I serve as Visionary and Pastor. With this assignment from God, the local church and community are my contexts and foundation stones for ministry. As I serve *ANLBC* as Pastor, our mission, vision, and creed are clear. We are to live to "Make every contact count for the cause of Christ." In doing so, service and outreach are the focuses of the church. We take to heart Jesus' mandate as found in Matthew 25:40, "And the king will answer them, 'Truly I tell you, just as you did it to one of the least of these who are members of my family, you did it to me'" (NRSV)[2]

Our charge, mission, and heart for service are for "the least of these," i.e., they are for those persons whose voices have been ignored or silenced, those persons who have been marginalized, discarded or forgotten by the greater society. As Pastor in a local church, I still hear the voices that I may have missed earlier; hearing those voices now stimulates within me a great responsibility to lead in a way which can be a model for responding to the needs of others as not just something nice to do but as a dire responsibility.

Anointed New Life Baptist Church attempts to be a model church that is not only in the community, but is also *with* the community to address the issues of community care, economic development, social justice, and spiritual growth. In concert with other local pastors who need to be informed, equipped, and prepared to address pressing issues that affect our congregations, this model church can help to heighten the awareness of, as well as inform and train pastors on PTSD. Such ministry to extended clergy forums might offer other areas in which awareness can be elevated and practical applications can be offered to broaden the purview of the needs of our congregants, pulpit clergy, and faith-based communities.

Mental health issues, especially for those suffering with PTSD, are not widely addressed in many, if not in most, churches. The results of the research I have conducted support the need for training of clergy and pastors on this issue. The model offered in this project attempts to address the void that is so apparent in the training curricula offered to pastors. This model provides another resource to reach the target population that this project seeks to address.

---

2. Matthew 25: 40 (New Revised Standard Version)

The Problem and Its Perspectives

PTSD is another chasm to span in the periscope of the local church. This is a very personal issue for me, and it is one that informs the thrust of this project. It is a *"Call for awareness and education"* for pastors, clergy, and local congregations in order for them to deliberately address Post-Traumatic Stress Disorder. It seeks to inspire what can be done as a faith community in helping those who are suffering with PTSD to find healing and wholeness.

An article written by James Melvin Washington, *The Grace of Interruptions: Toward a New Vision of Christian History*, spoke to the upheaval and the hell tantamount to what my family and I have been living since 2005 when my son, who served in Mosul, Iraq, under Operation Iraqi Freedom (OIF), returned home with Post-Traumatic Stress Disorder.

It was the title of that article, *The Grace of Interruptions*, which captured my attention and spoke to my reality at that time. However, at the beginning of this reality, in the fabric of my family's tightly woven tapestry of love, unconditional support, and strong family connections, no one would have been able to tell me how this one thread would unravel against our family's stability. My son had always relied on a strong sense of community, a family's fortitude in the midst of crisis, and an undaunting belief that God is able. I watched in almost disbelief as this truth slowly began to erode in him.

At the beginning of this turmoil, I would not have described our experience as "grace" of any kind. However, after six years of walking with my son through this ordeal, the grace of interruption has afforded me the opportunity to embrace ways in which I can help him as well as others to cope, survive, and to give assistance to untold numbers of others who are struggling with PTSD.

This interruption of life, as we knew it, moved me toward "a new vision" of pastoral response. It is a response in which pastors can recognize, respond, and write a new paradigm for our military service members—veterans, and their families who have suffered and who are still suffering from society's lack of recognition and acknowledgement that PTSD is a problem that affects all of us.

In many instances, our soldiers and their families have been treated unfairly and have been denied the services and compensation that are or that should be due them. The military was unprepared for the number of service members returning from Iraq and Afghanistan with PTSD-related issues. There are documented cases in which service members have been dismissed with less than honorable discharges because of their inability to perform their required duties. Once dismissed (with or without proper diagnosis), many are left with no recourse for benefits and compensation.[3]

My son was one of those statistics. He began to show signs of depression, irritability, a sense of hopelessness, and despair. He sank into deeper and deeper depression. Untrusting of the Veteran's Administration and with no recourse for benefits, he turned to his pastor for assistance. However, his pastor was not informed, equipped, or trained with the proper resources to provide counsel or a referral around the issue of PTSD. The pastor—the supposed spiritual leader appointed by God, the person who my son believed could give him guidance for his wounded soul, as it were—turned him away, further compounding his disillusionment, frustrations, and feelings of abandonment.

As the victim of war, my son sought out his clergy to articulate and expound upon what he was going through in the torment of his soul. He was not looking for a diagnosis, but a safe place to wrestle with and reconcile the spiritual and emotional conflict of his understanding of who God was pre-Iraq, during Iraq, and post-Iraq. His spiritual understanding of God after experiencing the devastating realities of the brutality of war did not make any sense. The God he encountered during war as he watched innocent men, women, and children killed, maimed, and mutilated was not the God of his childhood memories or his adolescent encounters. My son was in need of *soul care. Soul care,* as I define it, is the facilitation of healing and spiritual wellness through a restored

3. Frontline, Public Broadcast Station. *The Wounded Platoon,* DVD. Directed by Dan Edge. PBS Distribution, 2010.

connection of core beliefs and a reconciled personal relationship with God.

My son was not alone. Research shows that 40 percent of military personnel and veterans will approach their clergy before seeking help from mental health professionals.[4] Pastors and clergy cannot afford to ignore the impending needs of those whom God has entrusted to their care for lack of understanding about PTSD. Pastors are called to minister to persons with issues of *soul care*.

PTSD, I suggest, should be diagnosed as a *soul care* issue just as much as it is diagnosed as a mental health issue. Spiritual symptoms of combat trauma include, but are not limited to, feeling abandoned by God; finding it hard to pray; doubts about core beliefs; anger toward God; no Spirit of thankfulness; feelings of alienation from church, friends, and family; loss of faith and hope; and no yearning for righteousness. As clergy, and especially as pastors, our calling is to help those who struggle with matters of the soul.[5] It is this need and cry from those who are suffering that has led me to address this void in the fabric of our society through the training of the pastor who is serving the local church.

Preliminary Research

After my son's initial need and the lack of whatever was necessary from his pastor in response, coupled with my own initial lack of knowledge about PTSD, I heard a voice crying out for help. I began to raise my own questions.

If I, a mother and clergy person, am missing this population of hurting persons in our midst, am I the only one?

What are the mental health professionals saying about the role of clergy and church in facilitating healing?

4. Weaver, A.J., J.A. Samford, A.E. Kline, L.A. Lucas, D.B. Larson, H.G. Koenig. (1997). What do psychologists know about working with the clergy? An analysis of eight APA journals: 1991-1994. *Professional Psychology—Research & Practice, 28* (5), 471-474.

5. Military Ministry, *Ministering to the Military: A Guide for Churches* (Military Ministry: Newport News), 9.

Are there any models, trainings, or workshops that are specifically tailored to pastors who want to understand more and promote a keen sensitivity in their congregations and communities?

Interested in gaining insight on other pastors and clergy responses, and their position on the plight of our service members and veterans affected by PTSD and their need for pastoral care, I surveyed a number of pastors who were attending the Hampton Ministers Conference, held at Hampton University, in Hampton, VA in June 2010. See Appendix A.

The following statistics and observations are noted:

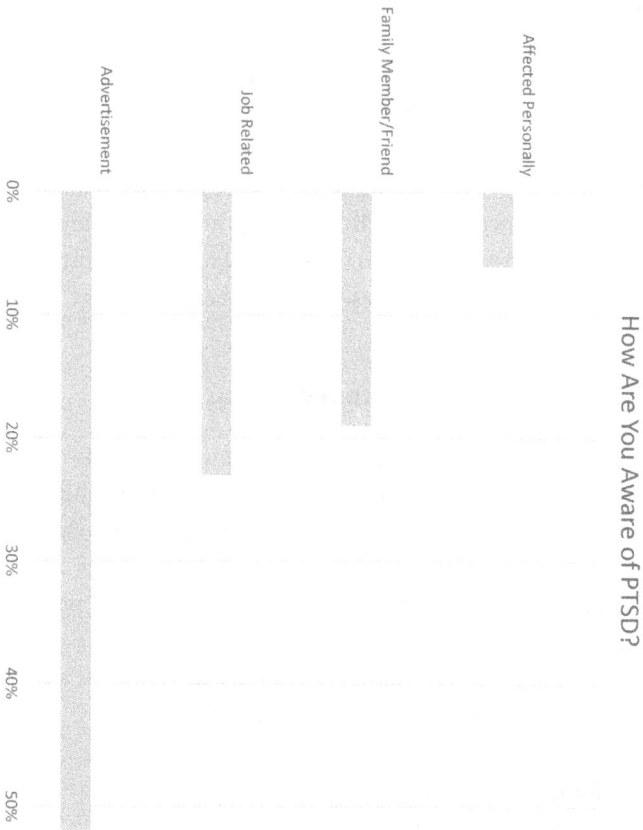

Table A. PTSD Survey Results, Question 1

The responses of ninety-seven pastors reflect that 52 percent of the pastors surveyed have gained their knowledge of PTSD from advertisements on television, in news articles, and in other public service announcements.

My research has shown that these advertisements provide general information on the existence of PTSD among the veteran population. But these advertisements do not offer detailed information to define and explain PTSD or the symptoms that are resident in those who suffer from it.

The next graph seeks to capture information on how pastors viewed the effects of PTSD on their congregations, community, and society.

The categories in this graph were defined as:

- State of Emergency—a systemic issue that affects everyone

- Isolated impact—a distinct issue that affects military personnel and their immediate families

- Minimal impact—a problem that has been well contained by military efforts

- No Impact—an issue that does not affect our society overall

- No thought—an issue to which no consideration has been given

When surveyed about the effects of PTSD on the congregation, community, and society, 38 percent viewed the effects as a state of emergency, while 29 percent had given the issue of PTSD no thought at all.

The responses from another portion of the survey show that 64 percent of pastors knew the number of active duty military in their congregations, while another 56 percent knew the number of veterans. However, only 2 percent had an active military ministry within their local congregation, and only 1 percent of the clergy who responded to the survey had any training on PTSD. Of those surveyed, 25 percent had churches within 10 miles of a military facility. Another 25 percent had churches 11 to 20 miles from a facility, and 39 percent had churches that were thirty miles or more from a military facility.

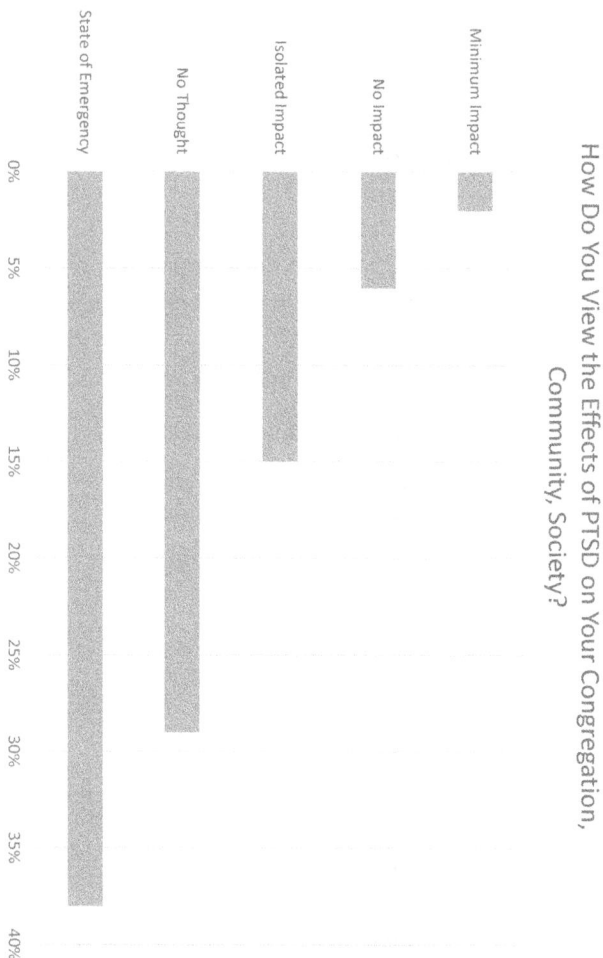

Table B. PTSD Survey Results, Question 2

Finally, 75 percent of pastors surveyed were interested in more information and training on the subject, while 25 percent had no immediate interest in pursuing the subject any further.

With 52 percent of the pastors who responded to the survey saying they received their knowledge about PTSD through advertisements, and 38 percent saying they viewed PTSD as a state of emergency, and, yet, 29 percent saying they had given the issue no thought at all, it became clear there was an urgent need for training. Everyone who participated in the survey had either active service members or veterans in their congregations. This gap speaks to the need for PTSD awareness and training among the clergy. The need for pastors to be sensitized, educated, and informed is vital to the well-being of our churches, communities, and families that have been entrusted to pastoral care.

An article released by the Associated Press and published in the *Army Times* states, "At the height of the war he escalated, President [Barack] Obama on Thursday declared major progress in turning back America's enemies in Afghanistan and Pakistan, promising U.S. troops will start coming home in July 2011. Even so, he predicted four more years of combat, soberly warning the gains could slip away."[6] Another article says,

> The recent military operations in Iraq and Afghanistan, which have involved the first sustained ground combat undertaken by the United States since the war in Vietnam, raise important questions about the effect of the experience on the mental health of members of the military services who have been deployed there. Research conducted after other military conflicts has shown that deployment stressors and exposure to combat result in considerable risks of mental health problems, including post-traumatic stress disorder (PTSD), major depression, substance abuse, impairment in social functioning and in the ability to work, and the increased use of health care services.[7]

With President Obama's initiative to return our service members home and the issues that accompany them from the aftermath

---

6. ArmyTimes, "Obama: U.S. on track in Afghanistan, Pakistan" (December 16, 2010) www.armytimes.com (accessed 15 January 2011).

7. Hoge, Charles W., Carl A. Castro, Stephen C. Messer, Dennis McGurk, Dave I. Cotting and Robert L. Koffman. (2004). *Combat Duty in Iraq and Afghanistan, Mental Health Problems, and Barriers to Care.* New England Journal of Medicine: 351, July 1, 2004.

of war, there has been an increased number of veterans in need of spiritual counseling and *soul care.*

An article by the Evangelical Lutheran Church in America entitled *"ELCA Congregations Prepare Care for Veterans Returning from War,"* states the point: "A great cadre of seemingly familiar strangers has emerged, 'strangers' who may be our neighbors, our loved ones, our friends, but nevertheless strangers as a result of brokenness they have experienced through the hell of war."[8]

The article goes on to quote Reverend Edgar W. Hatcher, retired chaplain, U.S. Air Force: "The truth is that war permanently changes the people who fight it. It produces tremendous moral and spiritual residue which impacts the veterans and their families. The church is a powerful force in helping veterans wrestle with and reconcile the love of God with the horrors they encounter and protect us from. Most pastors are woefully unprepared for ministry in these circumstances."[9]

With these alarming trends, I suggest that pastors must be open and willing to explore opportunities that will address the changes in the social and cultural systems that affect their congregations. In this way, we incorporate teachings that build up the faith community to relate to and value one another. In the process, we help to promote safe spaces for *soul care* and healing.

Pilot Presentation

As part of the needs assessment, I conducted a pilot presentation at the Annual Session of the American Baptist Churches of the South (ABCOTS) on October 10, 2010, in Richmond, Virginia. The class was a two-hour session with a fifteen-minute break. There were twenty pastors and other clergy in attendance.

In my PowerPoint presentation (See Appendix B) I addressed the following topics:

8. Frank Imhoff, "Congregations Prepare Care for Veterans Returning from War," The Lutheran, September 4, 2008, accessed November 9, 2010, http://www.thelutheran.org/blog/index.cfm?person_id=296.

9. Imhoff, 2.

- What is Post-Traumatic Stress Disorder?

- Statistics about PTSD and Its Sufferers

- Main Types of Symptoms

- Facts about PTSD

- The "Wounded Platoon"

- Military in Our Midst

- Challenges in Returning Home

- Raising Awareness of Pastors and Clergy

- Spirituality and Rebuilding Life

- Pastors and Community Response

ABCOTS conducted its own evaluation using a post- training questionnaire to assess the effectiveness of the session. Of the twenty pastors in attendance, fourteen completed the evaluation survey conducted by ABCOTS to capture the participants' thoughts on the seminar. See Appendix C.

Of the fourteen participants who completed the survey, ten noted that they strongly agreed that they gained useful information from the session, while four strongly agreed on the usefulness of the information, and no one disagreed or strongly disagreed that the information was useful. Thirteen strongly agreed that the seminar was easy to follow, while one agreed and none disagreed or strongly disagreed. Twelve strongly agreed that they would suggest the seminar to others, while two agreed and none disagreed or strongly disagreed. See Appendix D.

In further comments about the presentation, the participants noted (See Appendix E):

- "More time for information. Job Well done!"

- "I am hoping that we can get this info in our church."

- "Make this available to others in churches-at-large in the local area."

- "Excellent!"

- "Need more seminars at all Annual Sessions."

- "This seminar is excellent! The information priceless! Thank you so much for sharing your personal story. May God continue to bless you in your special ministry."

I contend from the voices of those who participated in this survey that we can no longer separate ourselves inside the hallowed walls of prestigious sanctuaries. Ministry must be relevant, but relevant ministry cannot take place without community. We have a responsibility as "Disciples of Christ" to emulate Christ and be among the least of these in order to address the needs of the most of these.

I maintain that our ecclesiology must be realized and accomplished through building relationships and sharing knowledge and resources. In all that the church does, whether preaching, teaching, fellowship, missions, or evangelism, it must be about building up people, bringing them into relationship with God through Jesus Christ, and liberating them from bondage. Thereby, the church is empowering them to find their full potential and live in fellowship as God commands.

The church is a dynamic reality. It has to be responsive to the demands of the times, for it must signify and represent the living God. Leading people toward this reality rests with the pastor, and his/her leadership and preparedness to respond to the needs of those entrusted to his/her care.

As I continue in the context of ministry as a church planter and serve as Pastor to address the needs of people and close the gap of this particular issue, I press to offer education, awareness, and training to assist pastors and churches to hear the cries of the people suffering with PTSD. I advocate for pastors to offer themselves as agents of change, and to watch as God heals one life at a time.

Chapter 2

Literature Review

In Search of Answers

IN 2005, AFTER WITNESSING my son's struggle with Post-Traumatic Stress Disorder, I began a personal quest to better educate myself. His wrestle with spiritual matters after serving in Iraq and living through destruction, devastation, death, and the violation of his moral truth, pressed me to ask questions. I inquired whether clergy serving in local congregations were either aware of PTSD or prepared to address, assist, or refer persons in their congregations who were affected by it.

At the time, there were many books written that addressed the psychological, behavioral, and clinical aspects of the ailment. What I found lacking in the dialogue of those on the forefront of exploration were the issues of *spirituality* and ways in which clergy could assist in addressing the concerns of those who are affected by PTSD. From my review of the available literature, there was limited dialogue and/or consideration on how local pastors and clergy might be another resource to facilitate the restoration and healing of those who suffer and who are challenged by the issues of the wounded soul and tormented spirituality. Pastors are called by God to minister to those in need in these two areas.

There have been any number of books, publications, articles, and journals written to provide insight on the cause, effect, symptoms, treatment, and even the disturbing statistics of the increase of service members and veterans who have been diagnosed with Post-Traumatic Stress Disorder. The findings from my research reflect that little has been written, developed, or offered as a reference or module for training that will seek to raise the awareness of this issue for those, whom I believe, are on the front line of intervention for many sufferers.

Oftentimes, those who suffer describe themselves as lost, empty, spiritually dead, and depleted. This description of the sufferers' view of their spirituality and the condition of their soul is not foreign.

In his book, *The Post-Traumatic Stress Disorder Sourcebook: A Guide to Healing, Recovery and Growth*, Glenn R. Schiraldi, PhD provides a comprehensive explanation of PTSD basics and explains how the American Psychiatric Association uses the Diagnostic and Statistical Manual of Mental Disorders (DSM) in defining PTSD from a clinical perspective. Dr. Schiraldi's approach helps to engage the reader to understand PTSD from the sufferers' point of view. Through the use of the *"Humpty Dumpty"* nursery rhyme, sufferers report feelings of being:

- "Shattered, broken, wounded, ripped or torn apart
- Like they will never be put back together again
- Bruised to the soul, devastated, fallen apart, crushed
- Shut down, beaten down, beaten up
- Nothing seems sacred or special anymore
- As though they are in a deep black hole, damaged, ruined
- Different from everybody else
- As though they are losing their mind, going crazy, doomed
- Dead inside, 'on the sidelines of life's game'"[1]

1. Glen R. Schiraldi, The Post-Traumatic Stress Disorder Sourcebook Second Edition: A Guide to Healing, Recovery and Growth (McGraw Hill: New York), 2009, 4.

Some would ask why service members and veterans see themselves this way. War and the trauma of war have always left a mark on the human spirit. Many who have survived testify to the horror of their war experiences. The threat of impending death, as well as participating in the death of another human being, often go against their moral upbringing, consciousness of right and wrong, and their spiritual understanding of a loving God. Though Schiraldi raises the issues and struggles of spirituality, he does not address or make reference to the role that clergy could play in this matter.

In the section of his book entitled *Aftershocks: When the Past Won't Stay in the Past,* Dr. Mark Goulston, MD, helps the reader to understand the different types of trauma. In discussing PTSD, he distinguishes between simple and complex trauma. Simple trauma can begin after a single event, such as one's experiencing a hurricane, a car accident, the death of a loved one, or sexual abuse. Usually, any one of these types of trauma responds well to basic treatments and cognitive behavioral therapy. However, complex trauma can occur when a person suffers repeated trauma.

Our service members find themselves very susceptible to both of these types of trauma relative to the Iraq and Afghanistan wars, especially with regard to multiple deployments and the constant fear of being put in imminent danger.

Goulston makes the following observation: "These chronic psychic wounds can change people, both emotionally and physically, in ways that differ from the effects of a single trauma. That's why survivors with complex PTSD often have more symptoms and require a wider variety of intervention than other people with PTSD."[2]

Goulston did not make a direct reference to the benefit this information could have on pastors and clergy who minister to their congregations. He suggested that having an understanding of the difference between simple and complex trauma would be beneficial in addressing the need in a context Goulston describes

2. Mark Goulston, Post-Traumatic Stress Disorder for Dummies: A Reference for the Rest of Us (Wiley Publishing, Inc: New Jersey), 2008, 29.

as "a wider variety of intervention." This wider variety of intervention can also help bring awareness that PTSD is not just a combat related illness. PTSD can affect anyone who has experienced trauma to the degree in which it has violated someone's personal boundaries.

Life After Trauma: A Workbook for Healing, written by Drs. Dena Rosenbloom and Mary Beth Williams with Barbara E. Watkins, provides a different approach for its readers. The approach is to provide a comprehensive workbook to those who have acknowledged their trauma issues. Designed as a self-help course, the workbook guides victims through the stages of trauma, with the goal of enabling healing and restoration through readings and exercises. The authors' intent is to deal with trauma in general, noting that there are some behaviors, reactions, challenges, and beliefs that everyone with trauma issues will experience. They state: "The long-term purpose of the book is to help persons recover a sense of safety, trust, control, self-esteem, or intimacy—whichever of these key areas in your life has been disrupted by trauma."[3] A number of the exercises were helpful in engaging thoughts about self, how trauma can affect, and how healing can be achieved. Nothing in the book spoke to the issues of spirituality, *soul care* or the healing of the silent wounds of war.

A voice that raises concern on this issue can be found in *Down Range to Iraq and Back*, by Dr. Bridget C. Cantrell and Chuck Dean. The authors provide a reminder of the brokenness of our soldiers who have engaged in the reality of combat and who must make decisions to live or to be killed. Cantrell does a thorough job in providing the reader with the history of PTSD dating back to accounts in World War I (WWI), World War II (WWII), and current wars.

The insight provided by the soldiers' accounts of leaving the battlefield, returning home and facing new and different challenges was riveting. Cantrell advises the reader that homecoming is a process, not a single event. She states her position in the following

3. Dena Rosenbloom, Mary Beth Williams, Barbara E. Watkins, Life After Trauma: A Workbook for Healing (Guilford Press: New York), 2010, 3.

way: "As soon as you set down in the USA it is easy to believe that your troubles are over, but do not let yourself get discouraged when life continues to unravel around you. Remember . . . it is normal to think differently and see life differently after spending a year in combat."[4]

Cantrell's description of the dynamics of the combat community and the soldiers' dependency on one another for companionship and survival helps to explain the difficulty in the reintegration process . . . Coming home for many is like leaving a part of your family behind, a concept many who have not served will not understand.[5] Though she offers many insights from the point of view of the soldiers' struggles, Cantrell does not speak to the emotional support that could be provided by the clergy and faith community.

Conversely, Edward Tick, PhD, in *War and the Soul: Healing Our Nation's Veterans from Post-Traumatic Stress Disorder*, speaks very candidly about the issues inside PTSD. His insight on the struggle of the soul speaks to the need of those who yearn to have a spiritual advocate. Whether that advocate is a pastor, clergy, chaplain, or therapist, sufferers need someone who can assist them in navigating the issues of reconciliation as they often feel separated from and abandoned by God.

Tick states: "Soul is what gives us our ethical sensibilities. It is *spirit* behind the 10 commandments, as distinct from the physical letters carved in rock. Soul is conscience."[6] He continues, "The soul is the drive to create and preserve life that of our own, other people, our community, and the planet—as we participate in the endless creativity of the universe . . . needless to say, war threatens to the utmost this imperative to create and preserve."[7] Tick paints a very clear picture; war is destructive. War kills, steals, and destroys

4. Bridget C. Cantrell, Chuck Dean, *Down Range to Iraq and Back* (WordSmith Publishing: Washington), 2005, 81.

5. Cantrell, 126.

6. Edward Tick, War *and the Soul: Healing Our Nation's Veterans from Post-Traumatic- Stress Disorder* (Theosophical Publishing House: Illinois), 2005, 18.

7. Tick, 17.

for many the part of consciousness that is imperative to our innate need to create and preserve.

This disconnect is reality for many of our service members who have dealt with the ravishes of war. In his prescription for healing, Tick offers that reconciliation can be had through the power of storytelling. "When we tell our stories, and listen to those of others, we come in touch with all three: life, divinity, and soul." Telling our stories, he declares, is a way of preserving our individual history while, at the same time, finding our place in the more global world.[8]

In his concluding remarks, Tick says, "The reality of war is horrible and deadly. When we try to turn the myth of war into reality to satisfy our craving for meaning and passion, we risk our own destruction, as well as that of each other and even meaning and reality themselves. PTSD is the soul illness suffered by individuals and cultures as a result."[9]

While I believe there is benefit in storytelling and shared experiences, it is my contention that safe spaces must be fostered for benefits to occur. It is through trusted relationships that this can be fostered more effectively. Tick offers a discussion on the value of the faith community's being a conduit to promote healing. However, Tick does not address or expound on how raising awareness or training the clergy to provide those safe spaces could be beneficial as another source for healing. To add, this is still another problem.

Hence, *Welcome Them Home Help Them Heal: Pastoral Care And Ministry with Service Members Returning From War* by John Sippola, Amy Blumenshine, Donald Tubesing and Valerie Yancey, was a helpful resource. It spoke to the issues of *soul care* and the clergy's role in understanding the dynamics of forgiveness, reconciliation, spiritual direction, and confessional dialogue to promote healing.

This resource identified spiritual maladies harbored by soldiers and the issues of the violated conscience. The perspective of these authors' position speaks similarly to that of the moral issues

8. Tick, 217.

9. Tick, 283.

of war and the effects on those with PTSD raised by Edward Tick in his book, *War and the Soul: Healing Our Nations Veterans from Post-Traumatic Stress Disorder*. The authors contend that "Spiritual well-being and the health of the soul are intimately related to ethics and morality. Any intentional perpetration of harm towards human beings, their livelihood, and their belongings can cause grave, moral injury and can damage the relationship to one's self, to others and to their relationship toward God. War unleashes massive, destructive internal and external forces that wound the soul and usher in moral failure."[10] The authors further share that "It is no coincidence that many veterans use religious language to describe the ravages of war. 'The war stole my soul.' 'I died spiritually.' 'I saw firsthand the monster in myself and in others.' The words 'soul,' 'spiritual death,' and 'evil' communicate an overwhelming personal experience of sin, concrete experiences of evil, and a profound separation from God, self, and others."[11]

While, *Welcome Them Home Help Them Heal* gives insight on the issues of spirituality and the soldier, it also suggests strongly the role of pastor in facilitating what can be offered to the congregation. It does not suggest how pastors equip themselves with training and education to better enhance their understanding of the issues at hand. Nevertheless, the book can be an essential tool for anyone seeking to work with soldiers and faith communities to promote reintegration and healing.

Ilona Meagher's book, "*Moving a Nation to Care: Post-Traumatic Stress Disorder and America's Returning Troops,*" is an excellent tool for anyone who wants to have a better understanding of the politics behind war. She provides insight, supporting data, statistics, personal accounts, stories of those affected, and of those who have been left behind to deal with the aftermath of war. The information on the impact of multiple deployments on our

10. John Sippola, Amy Blumenshine, Donald A. Tubesing, Valerie Yancy, *Welcome Them Home: Help Them Heal* (Whole Person Associates, Inc: Minnesota), 2009, 42.

11. John Sippola, Amy Blumenshine, Donald A. Tubesing, Valerie Yancy, 43.

soldiers, and the increased number of military suicides helps to put a face on the anguish many service members carry.

Meagher's is yet another voice that calls attention to the long-term effects of multiple deployments on service members and veterans. "To deal with the stress of multiple deployments, the San Diego Union Tribune reported in March 2006 that the Defense Department had been sending troops to war with a cache of anti-depressant and anti-anxiety medications."[12] As shown by this statement, the layers of the issues that service members and veterans experience are compound and complex. One "cookie cutter" form of intervention will not be sufficient to address the needs of those who are trying to navigate back from war into some sense of normalcy. Intervention will require the cooperation and collaboration of those who have served and survived, as well as those who can be advocates for the healing of the wounded soul.

Meagher affirms the following proposition: "The key to healing is to take hold of war's realities and use its lessons to give meaning to the trauma it creates. Political action and public engagement appeal to so many Vietnam (and now Afghanistan and Iraq) veterans because they help persons to come to terms with their wartime experiences. With their activism, they dip back into the current of life, serving as witness to the painful tide of war, while attempting to find personal salvation and release."[13] It is this release that speaks to the role of the pastor in aiding those whose voice has been quieted, marginalized, or stifled to find a seat at the table of justice so that their voices are heard. Intervention starts with an investment in understanding their plight and knowing what can be offered to assist those who suffer to be able to stand.

Meagher does not address the role of the pastor or of the faith community. However, this book is an essential tool to understand the cost of war, the government's political position on PTSD, and the need for advocacy for our soldiers and veterans to receive just and due compensation, health care and benefits. Offered in this

12. Ilona Meagher, *Moving a Nation to Care: Post-Traumatic-Stress Disorder and America's Returning Troops* (New York: IG Publishing), 2007, 88.

13. Meagher, 128

resource is a comprehensive chart of statistics for the Global War on Terrorism (GWOT).

Another resource, *Risking Connection in Faith Communities: A Training Curriculum for Faith Leaders Supporting Trauma Survivors* by Jackson H. Day, Elizabeth Vermilyea, Jennifer Wilkerson, and Esther Giller, is a helpful tool to anyone who is interested in facilitating training for faith communities on the issues of interpersonal trauma and healing.

This comprehensive curriculum offered by the Sidran Institute gives thoughtful insight and offers help to those who experience trauma at the hands of someone else, i.e., rape, murder, sexual assault, domestic violence, clergy abuse, etc. It also offers useful help to clergy who are assisting persons through pastoral counseling in a number of related areas. However, the authors make it clear that while individuals may find benefit from the curriculum in addressing other types of trauma, such as current, (as opposed to past trauma); national disasters, rather than interpersonal trauma; community trauma as opposed to individual trauma; those types of trauma are not the focus or intent of the curriculum.

The section on Spiritual Connection and Trauma was especially helpful in providing a more in-depth view of the clergy's role in fostering *soul care* to wounded congregants' spiritual connection with God. The section speaks to the relationship of trauma and spiritual distress, as well as disrupted spiritual beliefs and needs. It offers insight into how spirituality can promote healing. It is noted: "Western health providers, with their increasing wealth of scientifically-based knowledge and technical advances, have focused on symptoms rather than the whole person. Spirituality, no longer a primary cohesive element of American society, had generally not been considered an important element in planning and treatment of physical, emotional, and psychological problems. Fortunately, significant advances have been made since the 1980s, but survivors may come to you with spiritual issues that mental health providers are not addressing."[14]

14. Jackson H. Day, Elizabeth Vermilyea, Jennifer Wilkerson, Esther Giller, *Risking Connection In Faith Communities: A Training Curriculum for Faith*

In speaking to the need of the faith communities' involvement, the authors submit that faith communities are excellent resources for healing spirituality. The traditions of our forefathers bear witness to a spiritual connection with God that fostered in and for us wisdom about a personal relationship and connection with God. This wisdom teaches how numerous obstacles to spirituality can be removed.[15]

The authors also provide insight on the need for collaboration and extending clergy involvement, and they speak of the impact clergy will have by preparing congregations to be partners as caregivers. The authors warn that clergy who try to provide pastoral counseling without assistance might run the risk of burnout. The authors suggest that clergy should prepare congregations to understand their role as caregivers and to know how to contribute in the well-being of those who suffer from trauma. The authors contend that "Healing communities advocate open communities rather than condoning silence. Healing communities affirm and validate trauma survivors, in contrast to the larger so-called society, which often denies the existence of problems and stigmatizes the people who have them."[16]

In addition, "Naming the issue and acknowledging that it is widespread breaks the wall of silence and encourages affirmation of those who have experienced trauma."[17] It is these types of safe spaces within local congregations that pastors and clergy can create. Raising their awareness and educating them on the need becomes a win-win for all. The person suffering finds a place of solace. Those who facilitate gain a greater level of understanding and sensitivity.

The authors exhibited a thoughtful understanding of the role of the pastor and clergy in facilitating the process of healing by addressing the spiritual needs of both the sufferer and the faith

Leaders Supporting Trauma Survivors (Sidran Institute Press: Maryland), 2006, 56.

15. Day, Vermilyea, Wilkerson, Giller, 106.

16. Day, Vermilyea, Wilkerson, Giller, 106.

17. Day, Vermilyea, Wilkerson, Giller, 108.

community. Though this curriculum was not specifically written for sufferers of PTSD, it is an invaluable resource to use for understanding and training on trauma. Several of the case studies on *Spirituality and Trauma: A Scriptural Case* may be useful in pastoral care by clergy.

Other voices raising concern about the well-being of the soul are Nicholas Cooper-Lewter and Henry H. Mitchell in their book, *Soul Theology: The Heart of American Black Culture*. The authors provide a noteworthy perspective on theology and therapy in an extensive look at the belief system of Black people, and the healing found in Black oral tradition. Through clinical case studies they address a pattern of belief and life that heals minds and spirits. They contend, "Among oppressed people and all others under major stress, belief systems give healing and empowering support to psychic and spiritual survival.[18]

The authors showed a profound understanding of the need for balance between core beliefs and a belief in the providence of God as an integral and sustaining part of survival when dealing with trauma events and issues in life.

Most interesting in their work was their position on emotional balance. They state, "People keep or lose healthy emotional balance according to the adequacy or weakness of their core belief systems. Whether inside or outside the formally gathered churches, people's deepest belief about God will usually heavily influence if not outright determine their mental illness or well-being."[19]

While this work does not speak specifically to the issues of Post-Traumatic Stress Disorder, the case studies speak to the issues of persons affected by trauma, and the challenges they face in managing the complexities of life. The authors provide insight on soul issues as they relate to the need for understanding the dynamics of forgiveness, reconciliation, spiritual direction, and confessional dialogue.

---

18. Nicholas Cooper-Lewter, Henry H. Mitchell, *Soul Theology: The Heart of American Black Culture* (Abingdon Press: Nashville), 1991, 17.

19. Cooper-Lewter, Mitchell, 155.

There is a similarity to the position of Edward Tick, i.e., those who struggle with issues of the soul yearn to have a spiritual advocate who can help them navigate the issues of reconciliation, as they often feel separated and abandoned by God. The authors of this work offer the need for spiritual advocacy in navigating the healing process through theology and therapy.

This book is a solid resource for anyone desiring to expand their understanding of the Black culture and soul theology in light of trauma experiences, and how they can work hand-in-hand to facilitate positive results in mental health and healing.

Ministering to the Military: A Guide for Churches, by Military Ministry, a Division of Campus Crusade for Christ International, offers another essential tool that is helpful in identifying the military in our midst, their challenges, and what the faith community can do to help. Offered as a guide to help those who seek to understand PTSD, its effects on the soldier/veteran and the family, the authors provide valuable resources for assisting churches to begin to acknowledge, affirm, and support the military in their congregations and communities. They offer several links to training seminars on healing, marriage, wives, reintegration, as well as a DVD on training counselors, pastors, and lay persons. Though the information is helpful, it does not offer a training curriculum or module for *soul care* and spirituality on PTSD for pastors.

Along with the books, there were numerous helpful journals and articles. Many of them provided data, statistics, and insight on the rising numbers of soldiers and veterans who are sufferers of PTSD. Many offered statistics on the rise in domestic violence, suicide, substance abuse, and issues with law enforcement that are problems for many of our military and their families.

Military Pathways (formerly the Mental Health Self-Assessment), in the August 2010 edition article entitled *Record Number of Suicides in June*, stated that the military in June 2010 had reported its highest number of combat-related suicide deaths in Afghanistan since the war began. It also stated that post-traumatic stress takes a village. The article provided helpful quantitative data on suicides, and the need for clergy and community support for this initiative to bring awareness to the growing number of combat-related suicide deaths.[20]

A report by the VA National Center for PTSD: Research and Education on Post-Traumatic Stress Disorder released *A National Fact Sheet* that was helpful in providing insight on the impact of PTSD on the larger community. The report states: "While PTSD does not cause violence, PTSD symptoms can lead survivors of community violence to have difficulty managing violent feelings or impulses. For example, people with PTSD due to witnessing or being directly exposed to community violence may experience any of the following disorders:

- Disturbing memories
- Flashbacks or nightmares
- Feeling indifferent to their own or other people's suffering
- Increased arousal, startle responses and hypervigilance
- Feelings of betrayal

and offers "helping religious, educational and health care leaders and organizations to set up relief centers and shelters and providing direct psychological services near the site of violence and providing education, debriefing and referrals would be beneficial."[21]

An article in the Journal of Religion and Health, entitled *Spirituality and Trauma: The Role of Clergy in the Treatment of Post-Traumatic Stress Disorder* was more than helpful in speaking to the role of clergy and the need for more in-depth and controlled studies to verify the usefulness of spiritual assessment and intervention in patients with PTSD. The article stated that there has been an increased awareness of the spiritual aspects of health and healing. According to the statistics provided, "5-11% of trauma survivors

---

20. "Record Number of Army Suicides in June," Screening for Mental Health, August 12, 2010, accessed September 9, 2010, http://www.mentalhealthscreening.org/enews/sosanni.aspx.

21. VA National Center for PTSD, "PTSD and Community Violence: A National Fact Sheet" *Research and Education on Post-Traumatic Stress Disorder* (accessed October 10 2010).

will go on to develop PTSD and given the spiritual challenges in the experience of trauma, patients could benefit from spiritual assessment and intervention."[22] The author of the article suggests that clergy could be utilized to perform such assessments. After an extensive exploration of methods, she concluded that both the literature and experiences of the clergy from the study suggest that exploration of trauma-related existential conflicts in patients with PTSD is beneficial.

The Journal of Traumatic Stress offers a brief report on Post Traumatic Stress, Mental Health Professionals, And The Clergy: A Need For Collaboration, Training And Research. The information offered in this journal addressed the need for a collaboration of clergy and mental health professionals in order to provide for the needs of those who suffer.

The report states: "Tens of millions of North Americans with personal problems seek the counsel of clergy. There is an absence of research on the function of clergy as helpers with the traumatized and on the psychological dynamics of religious coping among the traumatized. Psychological trauma presents the mental health and religious communities with unique opportunities to work together in the best interest of those they serve."[23]

An article published by Pastoral Psychology, Psychological trauma: What clergy need to know, and written by Andrew Weaver, addressed the need for clergy to be better informed regarding the assessment and treatment of PTSD. Weaver suggests, "In a society that is marked by unprecedented levels of violence and a growing shortage of mental health services, clergy are increasingly confronted with situations involving psychological trauma that require expert crisis intervention skills."[24] This article offered spe-

22. Judith A. Sigmund, "Spirituality and Trauma: The Role of Clergy in the Treatment of Posttraumatic Stress Disorder." *Journal of Religion and Health* (Volume 42, Number 3), 221-229.

23. Andrew J. Weaver, Harold G. Koenig and Frank M. Ochberg, "Posttraumatic stress, mental health professionals, and the clergy: A need for collaboration, training and research." *Journal of Traumatic Stress* (Volume 9, Number 4), 847-856.

24. Andrew J. Weaver, "Psychological trauma: What clergy need to know."

cific and concrete guidelines for clergy who need a more in-depth understanding of PTSD.

A RAND report from the Center for Military Health Research published in 2008, notes the large gap between the need for mental health services and the use of those services among service members and veterans. The pattern stems from many critical incidences, and that pattern raises issues of the stigma attached to seeking mental health assistance. The RAND report states: "For example, military service members report barriers to seeking care that are associated with fears about the negative consequences of using mental health services."[25] Their survey suggests that most of those concerns center around the issues of confidentiality and career issues. "Many felt that seeking mental health care might cause career prospects to suffer or co-workers' trust to decline."[26]

There are many reasons why service members and veterans do not seek help when dealing with PTSD, but one of the more prevalent issues concerns the stigmas that may be attached to a mental health diagnosis. The Department of Defense and the Department of Veterans Affairs have acknowledged that this issue of stigmas reaches beyond what they can handle and that many veterans seek care through private, employer-sponsored health care plans and in the public sector in general. There is still a population that will seek counsel from the clergy; yet little is being offered in support of that type of collaboration.

An article published by the National Center for PTSD by the United States Department of Veteran Affairs, affirms that "Historically, there have been differences between the beliefs of scientists and healthcare practitioners and those of the general population. For example, one study (2) indicated that only 66 percent of psychologists report a "belief in God." These differences in viewpoint

Journal of Pastoral Psychology (Volume 41, Number 6), 385-408.

25. Tanielian T., Jaycox L. H. eds., "Invisible Wounds of War: Psychological and Cognitive Injuries. Their Consequences, and Services to Assist Recovery" (Santa Monica, CA: RAND Corporation, MG-720-CCF), 2008, 492 pp., available at http://veterans.rand.org, (accessed July 12, 2011).

26. Tanielian, 3.

may contribute to the lack of research on spirituality. The beliefs and training experiences of practitioners may also influence whether and how spirituality is incorporated into therapy."[27]

Addressing the Need

While many of the aforementioned books, publications, periodicals, and newspaper articles added to my understanding and knowledge of PTSD, there is still a void in the material offered for pastors, clergy, and faith communities. Though much of the material reviewed addressed the *who*, *what*, and *why* of PTSD, its effect on the soldier/veteran, families and the faith community, it does not speak to the pastor's role as the bridge to spiritual healing. The current material does not offer a curriculum or training module to address the gap within the role which the pastor offers as spiritual advocate and *soul care* provider to the local congregation.

It is my position that if healing, restoration, and reintegration of soldiers, veterans, and their families are going to be accomplished, and the soul wounds addressed, pastors of local congregations must be sensitized, trained, and educated on the needs of those in trauma. "When the War Comes Home with Post-Traumatic Stress Disorder: What Pastoral Leaders Need to Know" is a two-hour training session designed for this purpose. Offered by C. Diane Mosby, the training provides education on the symptoms, noted struggles, and issues of *soul care* for those who are suffering with this ailment.

I contend that the training will equip pastors with necessary knowledge, awareness, and resources to assist with intervention and guidance on issues of *soul care* and spirituality. I suggest that this model addresses a missing resource—the collaboration of psychological and clinical resources to equip another population of interveners: pastors. This collaboration can assist in addressing the

27. National Center for PTSD, *Spirituality and Trauma: Professionals Working Together*,http://www.ptsd.va.gov/professional/pages/fs-spirituality. asp. 1, Created April 11, 2011, Accessed July 12, 2011.

healing process from a spiritual perspective by enabling the pastor to be able to provide *soul care.*

This *soul care* which provides assistance with core beliefs, reconciliation with God, and renewed relationships with church and community can be achieved only when pastors and clergy are made more aware of the challenges of those in their congregations and communities, and are given the tools and resources to address those needs with training, information, and/or referral.

Once sensitized through training, literature, and dialogue to the plight of persons in our communities suffering with PTSD, pastors will be able to provide a conduit to help those sufferers by helping others to be more compassionate and understanding of the issues that confront those who suffer.

Chapter 3

Theoretical Foundations
for The Model

*(1) The hand of the Lord came upon me, and he brought
me out by the spirit of the Lord and set me down in the
middle of the valley; it was full of bones. (2) He led me
all around them; there were very many lying in the valley,
and they were very dry. (3) He said to me, "Mortal man,
can these bones live?" I answered, "O Lord God you know."
(4) Then he said to me, "Prophesy to the bones and say to
them: O dry bones, hear the word of the Lord" (Ezekiel
37:1-4 NRSV).*

Theological Vision and Biblical Paradigms

SINCE ANTIQUITY, GOD HAS been calling on those to whom He
gave prophetic messages to stand in the midst of injustice, adver-
sity, and ridicule; to see things, to speak things, as well as to speak
to things that were not as if they were. God speaks to Ezekiel as he
looks over the dry bones and asks, "Mortal man, can these bones
live again?" At first consideration of God's question to Ezekiel, one
expects the inquiry to be about the condition and ability of the
bones to be restored to life. However, a closer look leads one to
explore God's questioning of Ezekiel, and his belief in what God

is able and capable of doing. In essence, "Mortal man do you believe?"

The challenge for Ezekiel is to see beyond a present reality of hopelessness, despair, and disillusionment, and to visualize a future of promise, restoration, healing, and ultimately new life for the bones, regardless of their current condition.

As the prophet Ezekiel was commissioned by God to speak life into dead situations, so it is with the local pastor of the church today.

Ezekiel 37:1-4 reminds us that the role of the spiritual leader is to be able to envision a different reality for those who are despondent, depressed, and in despair. It is incumbent that the pastor has a word of hope and help for those who are seeking healing and restoration toward a brighter future.

In the current landscape of the twenty-first century, one area in need of restoration is that of persons who suffer with Post-Traumatic Stress Disorder (PTSD), especially veterans of the Armed Forces. Those who suffer from this syndrome often refer to themselves as useless, hopeless, and despondent, especially after encountering the aftermath of war. Many suffer due to no fault of their own.

Those who suffer through the pains and symptoms of PTSD tend to call upon pastors to walk through the valley of difficult times with them. Pastors are generally viewed as, or are perceived to be, a viable source that can offer good news to persons who are hurting, distraught, and disillusioned.

It is the pastors whom God has called in the twenty-first century to carry the prophetic message of hope, healing, and new life for those He has entrusted to their care. "Mortal man, can these bones live?"

Such a question is important because, like the prophet Ezekiel who has to believe the bones could live before God could use him to speak life to those dead, dry, and desolate bones, pastors of today also have to believe. Pastors must believe that when the plight of humanity, and in particular, the plight of persons with PTSD, appears dead, hopeless, and beyond restoration, God can use them to speak life and provide assistance in the restoration process.

The question to Ezekiel was not about the afterlife or resurrection, but whether it was possible to return to the world of the living where they see themselves as restorable. It is the same question for pastors today, "Mortal man do you believe?" Do you believe it is possible for persons with PTSD to return to the world of the living where they can see themselves as restorable? In order for this work of restoration to be effective, the agent of God, the pastor, must believe.

Post-Traumatic Stress Disorder has been diagnosed as an anxiety disorder, the result of which is trauma from certain exposures. It is a common reaction to an abnormal event; however, symptoms of PTSD may not emerge immediately after the traumatic event. It can be weeks, months, or even years before the symptoms develop.[1]

Meagher in her work, *Moving a Nation to Care*, explains: "PTSD leaves an unpleasant impression on the mind, like a scratch on an old vinyl record, which can cause permanent damage over time if left untreated. Dr. Edward Tick, a clinical psychotherapist with extensive experience in treating veterans, refers to combat PTSD as "frozen war consciousness."[2] Time appears to stand still as the trauma survivors skip repeatedly to the event(s) through intrusive thoughts, nightmares, and other triggers. Each repeat experience leaves the sufferers mentally and physically drained, and their anxiety and frustration increase as they continually feel out of control."[3]

Inasmuch as PTSD is a diagnosed mental issue, it is just as much a *soul issue*. Many persons affected feel no connection to God or have a fractured relationship with God. Deep physical,

1. Glen R. Schiraldi, *The Post-Traumatic Stress Disorder Sourcebook: A Guide to Healing, Recovery, and Growth* (McGraw: New York), 2009, 13.

2. Edward Tick, War and the Soul: Healing Our Nation's Veterans from Post-Traumatic Stress Disorder (Theosophical Publishing House: Wheaton), 2005, 99.

3. Ilona Meagher, *Moving a Nation to Care: Post-Traumatic Stress Disorder and America's Returning Troops* (IG Publishing: New York, 2007, 22.

psychological, and spiritual wounds are all war-related issues that threaten the mind, body, and soul, causing any number of physical, emotional, mental, and spiritual challenges.

> When spirituality has been affected by trauma, many survivors speak about feeling dead inside, as if the experience destroyed their essence. They speak of despair and resignation, hopelessness, and irrevocable loss. These spiritual losses seem to replay themselves over and over, as if dying is perpetual, in the moment. When people speak this way, they do not talk of mourning; they are often still in shock. They are not only describing their feelings of pain and emptiness, but are also frequently talking about the death of meaning and purpose, the loss of connection with God.[4]

It is this place of desolate hopelessness in the valley of dry bones that God calls upon those with His healing message to understand the plight of those suffering with this syndrome, and to provide them with a healing balm for their distraught souls.

Historical Antecedents

To put this thought in further context as it pertains to veterans, the issues of Post-Traumatic Stress Disorder did not begin with Operation Iraqi Freedom (OIF) or with Operation Enduring Freedom (OEF). Statistics show that the psychiatric casualties of war date back as far as the beginning of time. The Greek historian, Herodotus, writing on the battle of Marathon in 490 BC, mentions an Athenian warrior who went blind when the soldier standing next to him was killed, although the blinded soldier "was wounded in no part of his body."[5]

---

4. Jackson H. Day, Elizabeth Vermilyea, Jennifer Wilkerson, Esther Giller, *Risking Connection In Faith Communities: A Training Curriculum for Faith Leaders Supporting Trauma Survivors* (Sidran Institute Press: Maryland), 2006, 55.

5. Ilona Meagher, *Moving a Nation to Care: Post-Traumatic Stress Disorder and America's Returning Troops* (IG Publishing: New York, 2007, 13.

There are reports of those who have served in every war and who have suffered from some form of PTSD; however, our greatest indication that has called for a response was for those who fought during and returned from the Vietnam Era. A declaration in a journal article published by the Veterans Administration (VA) National Center for PTSD, says,

"The estimated lifetime prevalence of PTSD among American Vietnam theater veterans is 30.9 percent for men and 26.9 percent for women. An additional 22.5 percent of men and 21.2 percent of women have had partial PTSD at some point in their lives. Thus, more than half of all male Vietnam veterans and almost half of all female Vietnam veterans—about 1,700,000 Vietnam veterans in all—have experienced clinically serious stress reaction symptoms.

The National Vietnam Veterans' Readjustment Study (NVVRS) also reports other problems associated with its PTSD diagnosis. The NVVRS says that 40 percent of Vietnam theater veteran men have been divorced at least once (10 percent had two or more divorces); 14.1 percent report high levels of marital problems, and 23.1 percent have high levels of parental problems. Almost half of male Vietnam theater veterans currently suffering from PTSD have been arrested or jailed at least once, 34.2 percent more than once, and 11.5 percent have been convicted of a felony. The estimated lifetime prevalence of alcohol abuse or dependence among male theater veterans is 39.2 percent; the estimate for current alcohol abuse or dependence is 1.5 percent. The estimated lifetime prevalence of drug abuse or dependence among male theater veterans is 5.7 percent; the estimated current drug abuse or dependence is 1.8 percent.[6]

The Vietnam War taught some difficult lessons about the personal and relational price of war, according to the authors of *Welcome Them Home: Help Them Heal*. They note that within six months of returning, 38 percent of married Vietnam veterans were divorced. Between 40 percent and 60 percent of all Vietnam

6. Richard A. Kulka, et al). *Trauma and the Vietnam War Generation: Report of Findings from the National Vietnam Veterans Readjustment Study* (New York: Brunner/Mazel, 1990).

veterans experienced persistent emotional problems. The number of those who died by suicide easily eclipsed the more than 58,000 who died in combat.[7]

It has been noted by the Rand Center for Military Health Policy Research that the outcome for those who have served in the Iran/Afghanistan wars will not fare any better. A major study in 2008 by the Rand Center for Military Health Policy Research found that approximately 18.5 percent (300,000) of U.S. service members who have returned from Afghanistan and/or Iraq currently suffer from PTSD or major depressions; and 19.5 percent (320,000) report experiencing a traumatic brain injury. It has been further noted that half of those who need treatment for these conditions will receive minimally adequate care. "The prevalence of these conditions is high and may grow as the conflicts in Afghanistan and Iraq continue. The systems of care for meeting these needs have improved, but critical gaps remain. Without effective treatment, these conditions carry significant long-term costs and negative consequences."[8]

With the rising statistics of our sons and daughters returning home with the ravages of war as a part of their psyche and an imposing threat to their livelihood, pastors must become more sensitized and responsive to the plight and the needs of those returnees. With 40 percent of military personnel seeking guidance from their pastor, local clergy, and church for help, it becomes a present reality that no one can afford to ignore.

It is noted that veterans do not feel comfortable, nor do many of them trust the Veterans Administration (VA) and/or other social services agencies. Seeing a member of the clergy is often less

7. John Sippola, Amy Blumenshine, Donald A. Tubesing, Valerie Yancy, *Welcome Them Home: Help Them Heal* (Whole Person Associates, Inc: Minnesota), 2009, 12.

8. Tanielian, Terri, Lisa H. Jaycox, Terry L. Schell, Grant N. Marshall, M. Audrey Burnam, Christine Eibner, Benjamin R. Karney, Lisa S. Meredith, Jeanne S. Ringel, and Mary E. Vaiana. "Invisible Wounds: Mental Health and Cognitive Needs of America's Returning Veterans." *Rand Center for Military Health Policy Research*. www.rand.org/pubs/research_briefs/RB9336 (Accessed 25 October 2010.)

threatening and has less stigma attached. It is viewed as engaging a known community resource.[9]

Research has noted some of the stigmas associated with PTSD as:

- Being seen as weak
- Unit leaders treating those affected differently
- Unit comrades having less confidence in you
- Causing harm to your career
- Embarrassing to admit
- Lacking trust in the mental health professionals[10]

Without raising the awareness of our pastors, clergy, and congregants to the issues of PTSD, and without providing proper training, they will, more than likely, continue to perpetuate the stigmas that are associated with the mental-health issues that accompany those who suffer the invisible wounds and the closed doors of healing.

PTSD is not just a war-zone issue. PTSD can plague anyone in society who has been exposed to a traumatic experience. There are many people in congregations who suffer from PTSD. They are survivors of rape, domestic violence, murders of loved ones, suicides of close friends and family members, natural disasters such as 9/11, Hurricane Katrina, and the Haitian earthquakes. Pastors, for lack of understanding, cannot afford to ignore the needs of those whom God has entrusted to them. Pastors are called to minister to persons, right where they are.

9. Weaver, A.J., J.A. Samford, A.E. Kline, L.A. Lucas, D.B. Larson, H.G. Koenig. (1997). What do psychologists know about working with the clergy? An analysis of eight APA journals: 1991-1994. *Professional Psychology—Research & Practice, 28* (5), 471-474.

10. Frontline, Public Broadcast Station. *The Wounded Platoon*, DVD. Directed by Dan Edge. PBS Distribution, 2010.

Pastors as Educators

In the theological framework that undergirds this model, God showed Ezekiel in his vision that the renewal of the dead bones in the valley was a two-part resuscitation. First, the needs of the physical were addressed as the bones were restored to corpses with no spirit. God then told the prophet to prophesy to the breath. *"Thus says the Lord God: come from the four winds, O breath, and breathe upon these slain, that they may live. I prophesied as He commanded me, and the breath came over into them, and they lived, and stood on their feet, a vast multitude."*[11]

Clergy, and especially pastors who are called to help those who struggle with matters of the soul, are responsible as agents of God and servants for God to help those who have been wounded and who suffer to foster a spiritual connection with God.

> In Christian and Jewish traditions, people of faith are empowered by God through a covenant relationship. "You will be my people; and I will be your God." God establishes the signs and terms of the covenant. God shares power with the people, allowing them to bring into the relationship their requests, complaints, gratitude, and sorrow.[12]

Nancy J. Ramsey, a pastoral theologian, speaks to the power and authority of pastoral care and offers Isaiah 61:1-3 and Ephesians 4:11-61 as a compound basis for pastoral authority. She offers the Isaiah passage to assist in the understanding of God's spirit being at work in those who are called to pastoral care for the purpose of redemptive transformation of the structures, systems, and relationships that deform and destroy human life. Coupling Isaiah with the Ephesians passage, Ramsey says, "Those who lead

---

11. Ezekiel 37: 9-10 (New Revised Standard Version)

12. Jackson H. Day, Elizabeth Vermilyea, Jennifer Wilkerson, Esther Giller, *Risking Connection In Faith Communities: A Training Curriculum for Faith Leaders Supporting Trauma Survivors* (Sidran Institute Press: Maryland), 2006, 54.

are authorized by the community in behalf of its ministry and witness."[13] "The normative vision that emerges from Isaiah and Ephesians suggests that power and authority in Christian communities are to be used in behalf of God's love and justice. Those virtues are guided by intentions to empower others, encourage mutuality, and enhance interdependence."[14] Therefore, raising the awareness of and educating pastors on PTSD is not an end unto itself; rather, doing so affords opportunities for pastors to be a conduit to equip the congregation and the community for the work of the ministry.

Part of a pastor's responsibility is for him or her to walk in the authority entrusted to him or her as an agent of God, and to speak truth to power and life to death. As noted by Robert C. Anderson, the role of the pastor is to equip, lead, teach, admonish, and evangelize for the sake of the Gospel. Anderson contends: "A certain degree of pulpit teaching will be helpful in developing an appropriate, caring attitude among the people of a congregation. However, the most effective equipping in this area will be done as the pastor acts as a teaching model—displaying a loving, caring attitude toward his or her flock, while exemplifying the way his or her parishioners should conduct themselves."[15]

Pastors are called to be leaders, consolers, counselors, and agents of change. However, they cannot lead others to be transforming agents if they, themselves, are ill-informed, uninformed, uneducated, and ill-equipped in areas that affect the society in which they live or serve. Psychologist Andrew J. Weaver says, "In a society that is marked by unprecedented levels of violence and a growing shortage of mental health services, clergy are increasingly confronted with situations involving psychological trauma

---

13. Nancy J. Ramsay, *Pastoral Diagnosis: A Resource for Ministers of Care and Counseling* (Fortress Press: Minneapolis), 1998,114.

14. Nancy J. Ramsay, *Pastoral Diagnosis: A Resource for Ministers of Care and Counseling* (Fortress Press: Minneapolis), 1998,114.

15. Robert C. Anderson, *The Effective Pastor: A Practical Guide to the Ministry* (Moody Press: Chicago), 1985, 158.

that require expert crisis intervention skills."[16] The crisis intervention skills to which Weaver alludes speak to the complexity of the pastor's role and the need for ongoing education and training in pastoral care and counseling to assist in equipping those who serve in this capacity.

Phillip V. Lewis shares this observation: "God's leaders must be dedicated to allowing Him and the Holy Spirit to bring about intentional transformation while endeavoring to help in the transformation of His church and people. That is what the Lord did with His disciples, and they redefined religion as the world then knew it.[17] Today's Christian leaders and I contend that pastors are called to do no less than to redefine religious dogma for the twenty-first century, and to be willing to meet the challenges of a hurting society, a changing environment, a hopeless people, and to work diligently toward completing the work the Lord has given them. By analogy, the last thing a fish notices about itself is that it lives in water, says Phillip V. Lewis.[18] As pastors and Christian leaders, we cannot afford to be oblivious to the environment surrounding us, or to the plight of humanity around us, or to the call of the hurting who are among us.

Change is a present reality in the landscape of the dry bones scenario in which we live. But, when change becomes more than our capacity to cope, it becomes a crisis. H. Norman Wright affirms the following thesis: " . . . And if anyone is ever called upon more than others to help during a time of crisis, it is the minister."[19]

PTSD is a crisis. It is how pastors as educators and leaders respond to this crisis that will assist in the outcome, to determine whether these dry bones will live again. For pastors who lead congregations, serve humanity, and function as agents for God to

16. Andrew J. Weaver, "Psychological trauma: What clergy need to know." *Journal of Pastoral Psychology,* (Volume 41, Number 6), 385-408.

17. Phillip V. Lewis, *Transformational Leadership: A New Model for Total Church Involvement* (Broadman and Holman Publishers: Nashville), 1996,14.

18. Lewis, 5

19. H. Norman Wright, *Crisis Counseling: A Practical Guide for Pastors, Counselors and Friends* (Regal Books: Ventura), 1993, 10.

usher persons from being desperate, struggling, hopeless, and life-less toward a new life-reality of wholeness, healing and restoration, it becomes imperative to search his or her beliefs and convictions, and answer the question: *"Mortal man, can these bones live again?"*

God asked Ezekiel, for God knew that Ezekiel could not speak life to the bones, especially, if Ezekiel did not believe that the bones could live again. Ezekiel, walking in pastoral authority and the belief that God could restore the dead bones of Israel, spoke life. The bones came back to life physically and spiritually as God used Ezekiel as an agent of restoration.

This may be a fitting parallel for the twenty-first century pastor. Those who have been *"called"* to carry the Good News must avail themselves to be informed and educated on the ills that negatively plague humanity in order that they may lead persons toward healing, wholeness, restoration, and new life as part of their *soul care*. They must believe that the redemptive, restorative work of God is possible and must be equipped to speak life to situations that appear to be dead.

Chapter 4

The Treatment for The Problem

Relevant Help

MY RESEARCH, LITERATURE REVIEW of current materials, and my personal experience, have made it clear that many of our veterans, service members, family members, and congregants seek out their local pastor first in times of despair and trouble. To this end, many are looking for good news in the midst of some bad situations.

My offer to assist pastors to become better equipped for the challenges that accompany persons with PTSD in local congregations is a training class on this issue. Such a class will allow pastors to be exposed to, informed about, and enlightened on the issues of those affected. For the attendees of the class, the training will provide an increased awareness and understanding of PTSD. It will also provide suggestions and additional resources on how pastors can be of assistance in addressing the needs of those who are suffering.

At the conclusion of this training session, pastors should be able to define what PTSD is and what it is not. They should also have an increased knowledge of the symptomatology, etiology, and therapeutics pertaining to this ailment, and, thereby, be better informed about the needs of the military, and post-military in our midst.

Moreover, with intervention and guidance from pastors who are willing to provide *soul care*, persons suffering with PTSD will be able to seek out and find help in another trusted community to assist in the healing process.

Instrumentation

Four instruments were used to collect data for this project, including a Participant Information Form, a Pre-test, a Post-test and a Post-training Interview Questionnaire, all designed specifically for this project.

Participant Information Form

The Participant Information Form has been designed to collect demographic information so that the same could be described accurately and adequately. The information requested from pastors includes gender, marital status, age, educational background, years in pastorate, and military experience. For matters of simplicity, most of the items on the form require choosing the most appropriate response. Provisions have been made for unforeseen or unusual responses by including an "Other" category for some of the responses. The inclusion of this form in the training program provided an opportunity to correlate the demographic information with the responses from the Pre-test and Post-test. See Appendix F.

Pre-test/Post-test

During the training, the pastors were asked to participate in a Pre-test and Post-test. The Pre-test was used to measure the pastors' knowledge of PTSD prior to the workshop. The Pre-test consists of nine items; it takes approximately ten minutes to complete.

The Post-test was used to measure the pastors' knowledge of PTSD after the workshop. The Post-test consists of ten items and takes approximately ten minutes to complete.

The hypothesis of this project is that the workshop would increase the pastors' knowledge of PTSD. The responses from the Pre-test and Post-test were used to measure the increased knowledge of those in attendance on the subject of PTSD. See Appendix G and Appendix H.

Post-training Interview Questionnaire

This project employed a Post-training Interview Questionnaire. Available participants were asked to participate in a one-on-one interview approximately thirty days after the completion of the training course. The interview consisted of thirteen questions and took approximately one hour to complete. The interview was used to measure each pastor's retained knowledge of PTSD after the training by having the participants answer again the questions from the Post-test administered during the training session.

The interview also assessed if any action had been taken on the part of the participant to share such knowledge with members of his/her congregation. Provisions were made for open-ended questions by including space for elaboration.

This process addresses the hypothesis of the workshop and was used to measure increased and retained knowledge of the selected participants for the interview. Pastors for the interview were selected on the basis of their availability and their role as pastors in a local congregation. See Appendix I.

The Process

On August 17, 2011, invitations to attend a workshop were mailed to thirty pastors. The workshop was held on Saturday, September 24, 2011, from 9:00 a.m. to 11:30 a.m., at the administrative offices of the Anointed New Life Baptist Church which, at the time, was located at 9291 Laurel Grove Road, Suite C., Mechanicsville, Virginia 23116. The thirty pastors were selected from persons I knew who served in the pastorate of local congregations. Twenty-nine of the pastors selected were from the metropolitan Richmond, Virginia area. One was from the Fredericksburg, Virginia area. He was selected because of his interest in the subject matter.

The intent of the invitation was to have pastors participate in a two-hour training session on Post-Traumatic Stress Disorder, with the goal of raising their awareness of the issues associated with this illness.

On September 10, 2011, an additional letter was sent to the same thirty pastors to remind them of the workshop and to follow up on their response regarding their attendance. Directions to the administrative offices of the Anointed New Life Baptist Church were included in the letter.

On September 24, 2011, the Reverend C. Diane Mosby facilitated a training session entitled, *"When the War Comes Home with Post-Traumatic Stress Disorder (PTSD): What Pastoral Leaders Need to Know."* Reverend Cholon Coleman, Associate Minister of the Anointed New Life Baptist Church, assisted with the administrative needs. She also audited the proceedings of the training session.

Post-training interviews were held for two participants approximately thirty days after the September 24 training. The objective of the interview was twofold. First, the interview portion was used to collect qualitative data that captured the impact of the training on the participants' awareness of PTSD, and their ability to replicate such knowledge to others.

Secondly, the Post-training Interview Questionnaire was used to assess the knowledge retained from the information presented during the September training session. The participants were contacted by telephone and email to inquire of their availability to participate within the thirty-day timeframe. Interviews were scheduled based on the participants' availability.

On November 10, 2011, invitations were mailed to twenty additional pastors to attend a training which was held on Saturday,

December 3, 2011. To expand the opportunity to reach pastors outside of the conventional U.S. mail system, Facebook and email invitations were also sent to the same twenty pastors. The intent of this invitation was to broaden the data sampling by having additional pastors participate in a two-hour training session on Post-Traumatic Stress Disorder with the goal of raising their awareness of the issues associated with this illness.

On November 27, 2011, an additional letter was sent to the confirmed participants to remind them of the workshop and to provide directions to the administrative offices of the Anointed New Life Baptist Church.

On December 3, 2011, the Reverend C. Diane Mosby facilitated a training class entitled, *"When the War Comes Home with Post-Traumatic Stress Disorder (PTSD): What Pastoral Leaders Need to Know."* Mrs. Carol Watkins, a contextual associate for this project, assisted with the administrative needs. She also audited the proceedings of the training.

Post-training interviews were held for two participants approximately thirty days after the December 3 training. The objective of the interview was twofold. First, the interview portion was used to collect qualitative data that captured the impact of the training on the participants' awareness of PTSD and their ability to replicate such knowledge to others.

Secondly, the Post-training Interview Questionnaire was used to assess knowledge that was retained from the information presented during the December training session. The participants were contacted by telephone and email to inquire of their availability to participate within the thirty-day timeframe. Interviews were scheduled based on their availability.

The Analysis

The Pre- and Post-tests included information for quantitative and qualitative data collection. Information collected from the participants' Pre-test and Post-test was used to compare their responses prior to and after the training.

Based on my preliminary research and outcomes previously documented in Chapter 1 of this manuscript, I have concluded that most pastors have some general knowledge of PTSD through various sources, such as advertisements, public service announcements, general publications, and personal history. Therefore, taking into consideration that all attending had some, but varying knowledge of PTSD, the quantitative analysis from the pre-tests and post-tests was used to measure the increased knowledge of the participants as a result of the training.

The quantitative data calculations were based on the number of questions answered correctly. Of the five quantitative questions, each question was weighted at 20 percent, for a total of 100 percent. The analysis compared the number of correct answers prior to the training (Pre-test) to the number of questions answered correctly after the training (Post-test) to determine the percent of growth between the two tests. The information was graphed to show the knowledge growth from the training.

Approximately 30 days after the training, four pastors participated in the Post-test again. This data was used to determine knowledge retained using the same calculation method.

A follow-up interview was conducted with four pastors who participated in the training. This qualitative assessment tool was used to determine the effectiveness of the training, retained knowledge of the participants, and their ability to replicate such knowledge to others.

Chapter 5

The Execution of The Process

THE RESEARCH METHODOLOGY FOR this project and the hypothesis were outlined in chapter four. The hypothesis suggests that the treatment (workshop) will increase the pastors' knowledge of PTSD, and raise their awareness of some of the challenges facing persons who are affected.

This chapter will further explore the direct correlation of the research methodology with the model application by recording the preliminary preparation, the execution of the treatment through the training session, and the observers' summarizations.

Preliminary Preparation

On August 17, 2011, invitations were mailed to thirty pastors to attend a workshop on Post-Traumatic Stress Disorder. The workshop was held on Saturday, September 24, 2011, from 9:00 a.m. to 11:30 a.m., at the administrative offices of the Anointed New Life Baptist Church. At the time, the church was located at 9291 Laurel Grove Road, Suite C., Mechanicsville, Virginia 23116.

The following Thursday, the Reverend Cholon Coleman, Associate Minister of the Anointed New Life Baptist Church, was asked to serve as observer for the workshop. She accepted.

Several days later, I met with Reverend Coleman to explain the role of an observer. She was introduced to the observation data collection model as outlined in *Designing Qualitative Research 3rd Edition* by Catherine Marshall and Gretchen B. Rossman (pages 107 to 109) as a guide for capturing her observations of the training session.

Two weeks prior to the workshop, an additional letter was sent to the same thirty pastors to remind them of the workshop and to follow up on their responses regarding their attendance. Through email I followed up with them again on September 19 to confirm their receipt of the letter sent on September 10, and to answer any questions pertaining to directions to the office.

On Friday, September 23, the Reverend C. Diane Mosby arrived at the administrative offices of the Anointed New Life Baptist Church (ANLBC) to prepare for the training session to be held the next morning.

In expectation of the ten persons who confirmed their attendance, the training room was set up to accommodate twelve participants and one observer. Preparing for twelve allowed for two unconfirmed attendees. The room was set conference style with seating for twelve around a large, oblong conference table. The LCD projector was set up at one end of the table for projection at the opposite end of the room. This arrangement was selected to allow the participants the ease of shifting their attention between the presentation shown on the projection wall and the facilitator's providing the training at the opposite end of the table.

A two-pocket folder of materials was prepared and placed in front of each seat. Paperclipped to the outside of the folder was the IRB Consent Form. The inside, left pocket of the folder included the Participant Information Form and the Pre-test Survey Form. A copy of the PowerPoint presentation to be used during the training was in the right-pocket. The copy included space for note-taking and comments. The folder also included several pamphlets on PTSD and additional referral information.

Coasters, bottles of water, pens, and candy dishes with mints, lozenges, and chocolates were placed in the center of the table. In an adjacent room, a continental breakfast of coffee, hot tea, water, juices, assorted Danish, fresh fruit, cheese, and crackers was available.

The following is the agenda for the training session:

9:00 a.m.—9:15 a.m.	Opening remarks and introductions
9:15 a.m.—9:30 a.m.	IRB Consent Form, Participant Information Form, and Pre-test
9:30 a.m.—10:15 a.m.	First half of the training session
10:15 a.m.—10:25 a.m.	Ten-minute break
10:30 a.m.—11:00 a.m.	Second half of the training session
11:00 a.m.—11:15 a.m.	Questions and answers period
11:15 a.m.—11:30 a.m.	Post-test and closing
11:30 a.m.—11:45 a.m.	Light refreshments

Treatment and Model Design

A PowerPoint presentation was used as a training tool. The presentation provided information on the following areas relevant to PTSD:

a. What is Post-Traumatic Stress Disorder (PTSD)?

b. Facts about PTSD

c. Symptoms of PTSD

d. The Military in Our Midst (Video clip by PBS/Frontline 20/20)

e. Challenges in Returning Home

f. Spiritual Symptoms

g. Spiritual Symptoms of Combat Trauma

h. Why the Need for Pastors and Clergy?

i. Pastors and Community Response

See attached Appendix J.

Several additional resources were distributed at the conclusion of the workshop. *Veterans and Families; Guide to Recovering from PTSD* by Stephanie Laite Lanham, provided additional information on PTSD for families and children. *The Federal Benefits for Veterans, Dependents & Survivors, 2010 Edition*, Department of Veterans Affairs, offered information on veteran health care, pension, insurance, and burial. *Post-Traumatic Stress Disorder (PTSD)*, McGuire Veterans Affairs Medical Center, Richmond, Virginia, included general information on symptoms of PTSD. The brochure, *Women Veterans Health Care: You Served, You Deserve the Best Care Anywhere*, Department of Veterans Affairs, described assistance and health care specifically for women veterans. The participants also received *Psalm 91: God's Shield of Protection*, Peggy Joyce Ruth and Angelia Ruth Schum, a devotional book based on Psalm 91, written specifically for veterans.

The Execution of the Treatment

The First Training Session

On Saturday, September 24, 2011, the facilitator, Reverend C. Diane Mosby, Mrs. Joyce Streater (who assisted in the preparation of the continental breakfast), and the Reverend Cholon Coleman, (the observer), arrived at the administrative offices of ANLBC at 8:00 a.m. to finalize preparation for the training session.

The first participants arrived at 8:55 a.m. At 9:00 a.m. seven of the ten participants were in attendance. The training session began at 9:09 a.m., with seven participants present, and the Reverend C. Diane Mosby as facilitator.

Reverend Mosby opened the session by thanking the participants for their attendance. She provided logistical information about the refreshments, bathroom location, followed by a brief overview of the day's agenda. The participants were introduced to Reverend Coleman as the silent observer for the day. Inquiry was made if any of the participants were veterans. One participant responded in the affirmative and was thanked for his sacrifice and service.

The participants were then asked to direct their attention to the packets in front of them on the table. The IRB Consent Form was explained with time for questions and clarity. Once the review was complete, participants were asked to grant their consent to be a part of the study by putting their initials on the front page and their signature on the last page. Once completed, the forms were collected.

Next, the participants' attention was directed to the right pocket of the folder. The Participant Information Form was explained, and the participants were asked to complete the form. Once completed, the forms were collected. Finally, the attendees were asked to complete the Pre-test. It was explained that the intent of the form was to assess their knowledge of PTSD prior to the training, followed by a Post-test after the training.

Once all the forms were completed and collected, the training began utilizing the PowerPoint presentation entitled *"When the War Comes Home with Post-Traumatic Stress Disorder: What Pastoral Leaders Need to Know."* See Appendix J.

Two additional participants arrived late and were asked to read and sign the IRB Consent Form and to complete the Pre-test Survey before proceeding with the presentation. Their arrival increased the attendance for the day to nine participants.

The first half of the presentation lasted approximately thirty-five minutes, covering the following areas:

a. What is Post-Traumatic Stress Disorder (PTSD)?

b. Facts about PTSD

c. Symptoms of PTSD

The participants were given time for a ten-minute break; however, they declined the break and decided to continue with the training without interruption.

The next portion of the training covered "The Wounded Platoon," a video clip by PBS/Frontline 20/20. An introduction of the video was provided. It was shared that some of the scenes in the video might be disturbing. Participants were encouraged to leave the room if at any time the video was uncomfortable to them. The training proceeded with the viewing of the video. Once completed, several participants engaged in an insightful discussion.

The final forty minutes of the training were shared around the areas of the veterans' challenges in returning home, the spiritual symptoms of PTSD, the spiritual symptoms of combat trauma, why the need for pastors and clergy involvement, and the pastors and community response.

Concluding remarks and closing statements were offered at approximately 11:00 a.m. The participants' attention was then directed to the Post-test, and they were asked to complete the survey. Once finished, they were invited to partake of the refreshments.

Several questions were raised and a number of comments were made throughout the presentation. Those questions and comments are captured in the observers' documentation. See Appendix K and Appendix L.

The Second Training Session

A second training was scheduled to be held on Saturday, December 3, 2011, from 9:00 a.m., to 11:30 a.m., again at the administrative offices of Anointed New Life Baptist Church.

On November 10, 2011, invitations were mailed to twenty additional pastors to attend the December 3 training. Facebook and email were also used to expand the opportunity to reach the same twenty pastors outside of the conventional U.S. Postal Service. The intent of this invitation was to broaden the data sampling by having additional pastors participate in the two-hour training session on Post-Traumatic Stress Disorder and raise their awareness of the issues associated with this illness.

On November 27, an additional letter was sent to the eight confirmed participants to remind them of the workshop and to provide directions to the administrative offices of the Anointed New Life Baptist Church. However, on November 30, notice was received that one of the confirmed participants would not be able to attend, leaving seven participants for the training.

Several weeks prior to the workshop, a meeting was held with Mrs. Carol Watkins to explain the role of an observer. The observation data collection model outlined in Designing Qualitative Research 3rd Edition by Catherine Marshall and Gretchen B. Rossman (pages 107 to 109) was used as a guide to show her how to capture her observations of the training session.

The day before the workshop, Reverend C. Diane Mosby arrived at the administrative offices of the Anointed New Life Baptist Church (ANLBC) to prepare the office for the training session.

There were seven confirmed participants. The accommodations were set up for eight participants and one observer. The room was arranged as it had been for the September 24 training. The materials included the same handouts and information from the previous session. The folders were prepared and placed in front of each seat.

Additional resources, to be given to each participant at the end of the session, were placed at the end of the table. The center of the table was set up with water, pens, candy, and coasters. In the adjacent room, a continental breakfast of coffee, hot tea, water, juices, assorted Danish, fresh fruit, cheese, and crackers was made available.

On Saturday, December 3, 2011, the facilitator, Reverend C. Diane Mosby, Mrs. Joyce Streater (who again assisted in the preparation of the continental breakfast), and Mrs. Carol Watkins, (the observer), arrived at the Administrative offices of ANLBC between 8:00 a.m. and 8:15 a.m. to make final preparations for the training session.

The first participants arrived at 8:45 a.m., and enjoyed refreshments while awaiting the other participants' arrivals. At 9:30 a.m., only two of the seven confirmed participants were in attendance. At the time of the beginning of the session at 9:35 a.m., three persons were present. The fourth participant arrived ten minutes later.

The session opened with an apology for the tardiness of the session's opening. Attendees were thanked for their participation and were provided logistical information about bathroom location, refreshments, and given an overview of the agenda. The participants were introduced to Mrs. Watkins and her role as silent observer for the session. Inquiry was made regarding any veterans who were participating. None of the participants had served in the Armed Forces.

The IRB Consent Form, the need for their agreement to participate in the training, and their signatures on the document were explained.

The participants filled out the Participant Information Form. Next, they completed the Pre-test. The intent of the survey was explained with the Post-test to follow at the end of the training.

Once all the forms were completed and turned in, the training began by utilizing the same PowerPoint presentation that had been used for the training on September 24. See Appendix J.

The first half of the presentation lasted approximately twenty-five minutes. Fewer questions were asked in the first section of the training than during the previous training session. The second group of participants also declined a break, and the training session continued.

The clip from the PBS/Frontline 20/20 video, "The Wounded Platoon," was introduced to the participants with the caveat that some of the scenes might be disturbing. Participants were encouraged to leave the room if, at any time, the video was uncomfortable to them.

After the video, there was a lengthy discussion on the content of the video. The participants raised several concerns about the symptoms of PTSD, the military's treatment of those represented in the video, and the stigmas attached to persons with mental illness, and other invisible wounds of war.

The final segment of the training was presented over a period of thirty minutes with great conversation around the struggles and inconsistency of assistance for persons with PTSD. Additional questions and comments were made throughout the training and are captured in the observer's documentation. See Appendix K and Appendix L.

Comment Summarization from Observers—First and Second Training Sessions

Reverend Cholon Coleman and Mrs. Carol Watkins served as observers for the trainings held on September 24, 2011 and December 3, 2011, respectively. Their roles included documenting the events of the training session and providing administrative assistance for the day. From their detailed documentation, a summary of comments was provided. They offered that the information presented was informative and insightful. The delivery of the information was balanced with facts and figures. Throughout the training, participants were engaged, nodding affirmatively, and actively thinking. The facilitator kept the presentation flowing and interesting. The facilitator's use of personal stories helped to put a face on the ailment. She also helped the participants to view PTSD in other aspects, assisting them in broadening their view of others affected. The video was an excellent resource. However, after viewing and discussing the scenes used for the training, the participants wanted information on the outcome of the persons affected by PTSD in the video.

In both workshops, no one was ready to leave, and both groups continued conversation around the training and the topic after the facilitator officially concluded the training.

Chapter 6

Project Evaluation, Findings, and Summary

FOUR INSTRUMENTS WERE USED throughout the project execution to collect data for analysis to accept or to reject the stated hypothesis. The hypothesis is to effect and increase the knowledge base of the participants, and raise their awareness of the subject of Post-Traumatic Stress Disorder. The analysis and results of this data follow.

Demographic Information

Thirteen participants attended the two training sessions. The Participant Information Form designed specifically for this project identifies the following demographic information:

Age Range of Participants

The participants were between thirty-six and sixty years of age. Five were forty or under. This age range had the highest representation. Four participants were between forty-one and forty-five years of age. Two were between fifty-one and fifty-five years of age. There was one participant in the forty-six to fifty age range, and one in the fifty-six to sixty age group.

The data also reflect a twenty-year age difference between the youngest and oldest participant. Conversations and observations during the training pointed out that the participants who were older than forty-six were more aware of the effects of past wars. They were especially sensitive to the outcome of the Vietnam War on our churches and society, more so than those who were in the

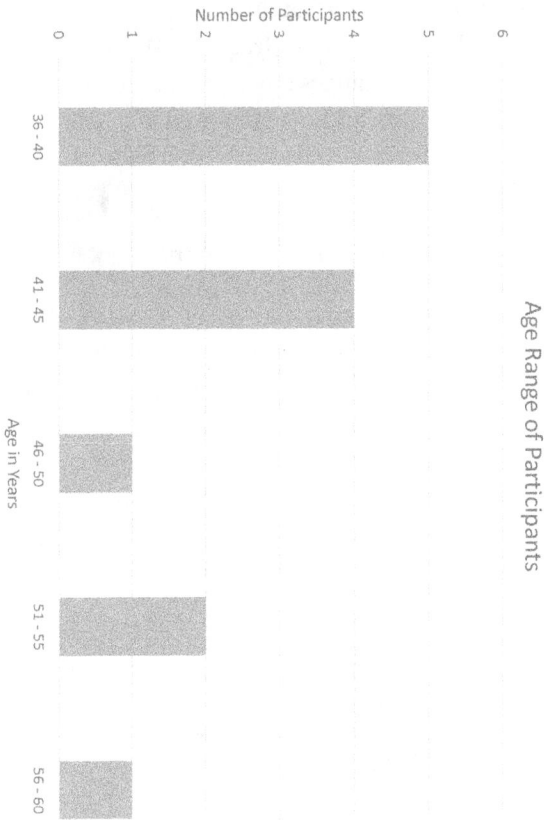

Number of Participants

Age Range of Participants

Age in Years

Table C. Age Range of Participants

thirty-six to fifty age group. Their conversations, led by a Vietnam War veteran, spoke to first-hand accounts of the military culture, stigmas, and the challenges of being properly compensated for service. Their conversations included stories of veterans they knew personally, and who had returned from the war with "shell shock," and drug, and alcohol addictions.

The younger participants (those between the ages of thirty-six and forty-five) spoke on these issues from a second-hand account, having heard family members talk of the experiences and challenges of addressing the needs of family members. By the conclusion of the training, additional conversations ensued on the effects of the current wars (Iraq and Afghanistan) on all age groups, stirring active conversations about the current experiences of people they personally know or have encountered who are suffering with PTSD.

Race of Participants

Of the thirteen participants, one was Caucasian. All the other participants were African-American. The result of the training reflected no visible or noticeable disparity of the impact of the information on the participants because of race. All the participants were actively engaged and shared stories of personal impact, tragedy, and the struggles of family members and friends who were or who are touched by the destructive nature of war. This speaks to the reality that war has no color, race or gender bias; it is a shared experience which affects us all.

Marital Status of Participants

Eleven of the participants were married. One participant was single (never married), and one was divorced.

Race of Participants

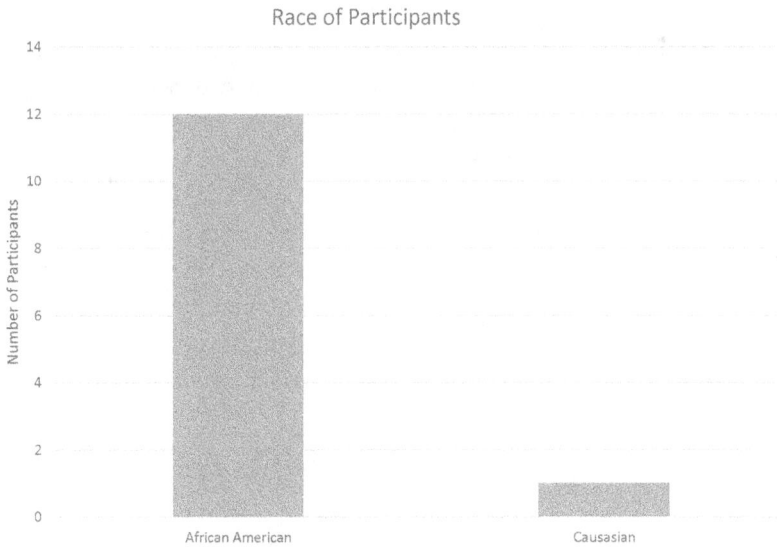

Table D. Race of Participants

Marital Status of Participants

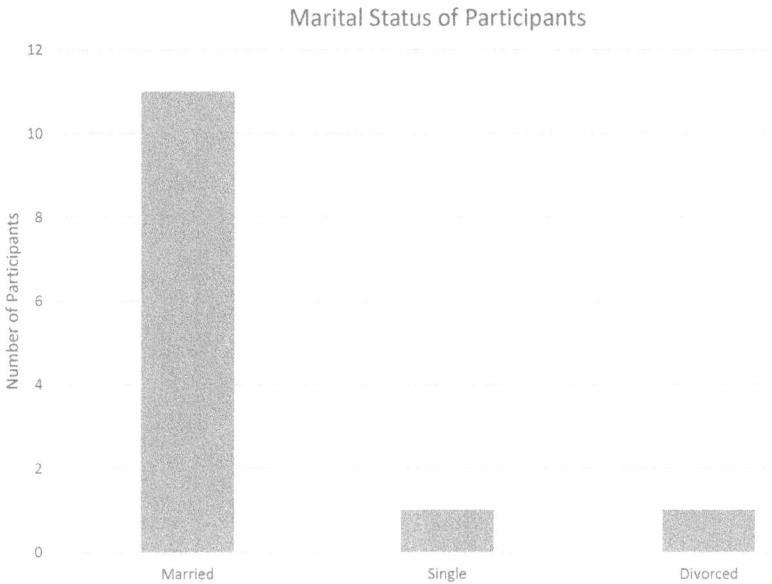

Table E. Marital Status of Participants

Gender of Participants

Of the total thirteen participants, eleven were male; two were female. The gender ratio of seven men to two women in the first training, compared to all (four) men in the second training changed the dynamic of the conversation and observation in the two sessions.

The session in which the women were in attendance brought more attention to the dynamics and effects of PTSD on the family and children, and the impact the issue has on the home and family at large. The class with all men spoke about the issues of politics, military culture, and expectations, as well as the need for change and social justice.

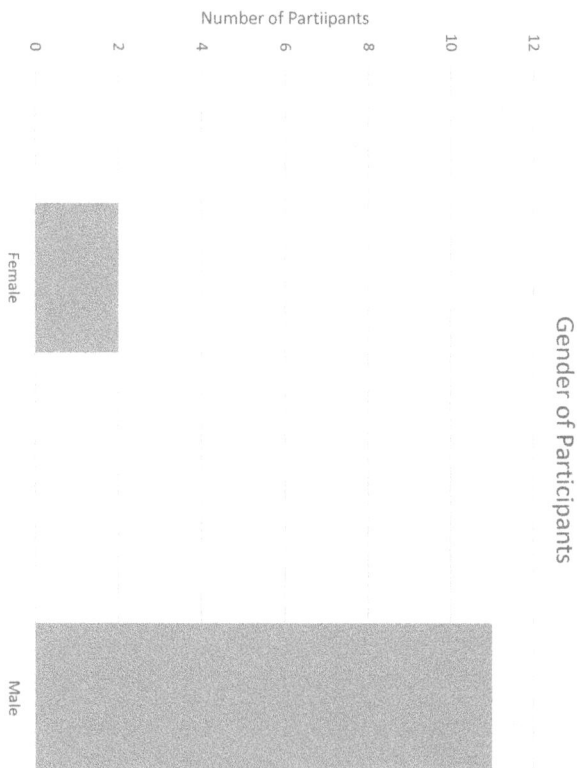

Number of Partiipants

0   2   4   6   8   10   12

Female

Male

Gender of Participants

Table F. Gender of Participants

Education Level of Participants

Nine participants reported having a Master's degree. Two participants had earned their doctoral degree. Two participants had attended college but had not obtained a degree.

There were no noted comments that addressed the demographics of either marital status or education. However, there was a brief discussion on the return of veterans to the academic campus. After completing their tour of duty, many veterans are now eligible for benefits under their Government Issued (G.I.) Bill. The question was raised whether college administrators had given thought to the concern for those veterans with PTSD returning to the college campuses.

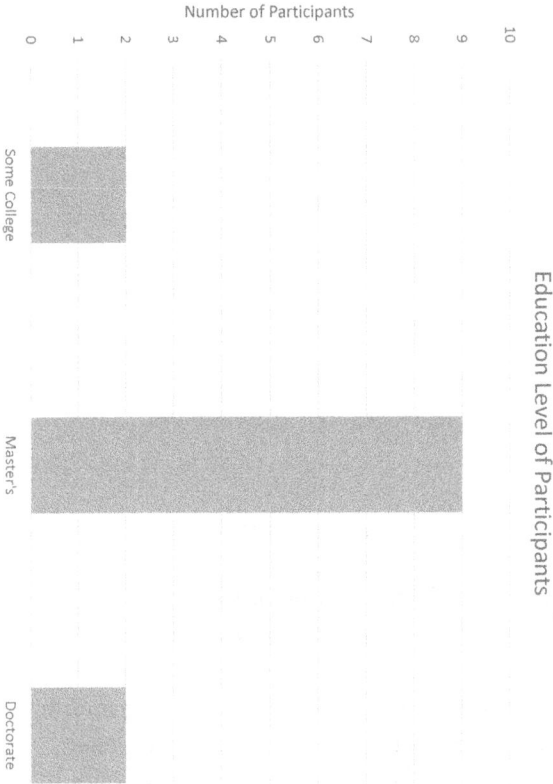

Table G. Education Level of Participants

Ministry Role of Participants

Among the participants there were twelve pastors and one church elder.

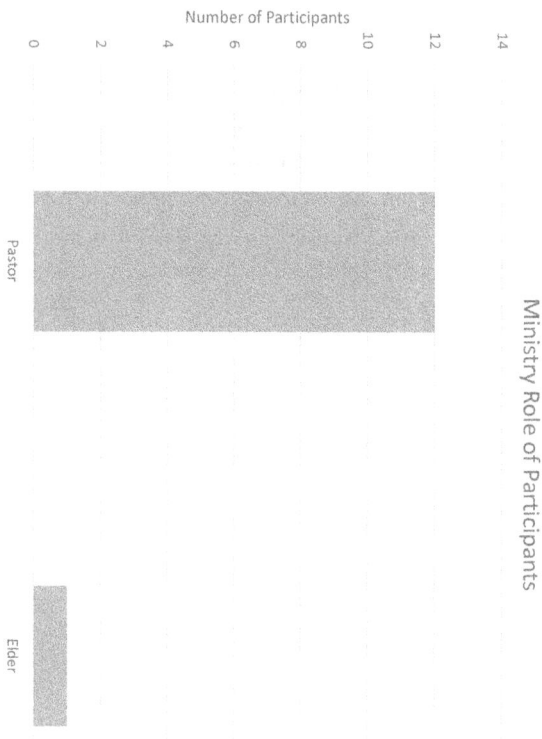

Table H. Ministry Role of Participants

Years in Ministry

Among the participants, six (the largest group) had served in ministry from one to five years. Three had been in ministry for sixteen to twenty years. Two participants had been in ministry twenty-one years or more. One participant had been in ministry six to ten years; another fell in the eleven to fifteen years range.

The result of the demographic data identifies that the participants were all pastors serving local congregations. This group was selected for their potential ability to effect change and address the need for the *soul care* of veterans and members of their congregations.

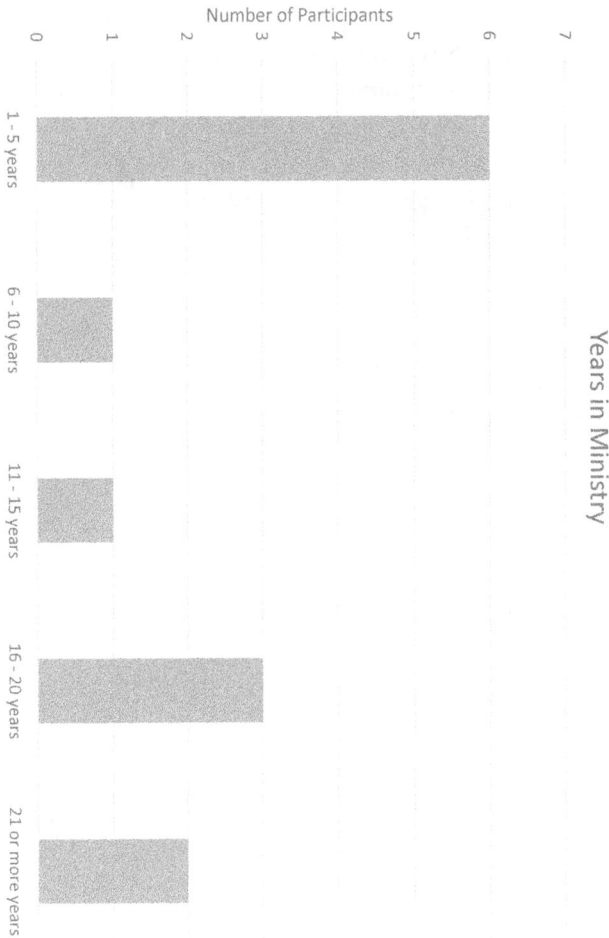

Number of Participants

Years in Ministry

Years in Ministry	Number of Participants
1 - 5 years	6
6 - 10 years	1
11 - 15 years	1
16 - 20 years	2
21 or more years	1

Table I. Years in Ministry

An interesting observation emerged regarding the years in the pastorate. The more seasoned pastors were more in tune to the spiritual needs of their congregation and the family dynamics. They spoke more candidly about the effects of trauma and the ripple effect that trauma has on the family unit. Coupled with the age demographic and the sensitivity of the more seasoned pastors to the Vietnam War, it appears they have been addressing the *soul care* issues of PTSD within their congregations; it just had not been named. Those with fewer years in the pastorate brought more attention to community awareness and the needs for more ministries in the church and community to address those needs.

There was one participant, a veteran who, served in Vietnam. However, none of the thirteen participants had ever been diagnosed with Post-Traumatic Stress Disorder.

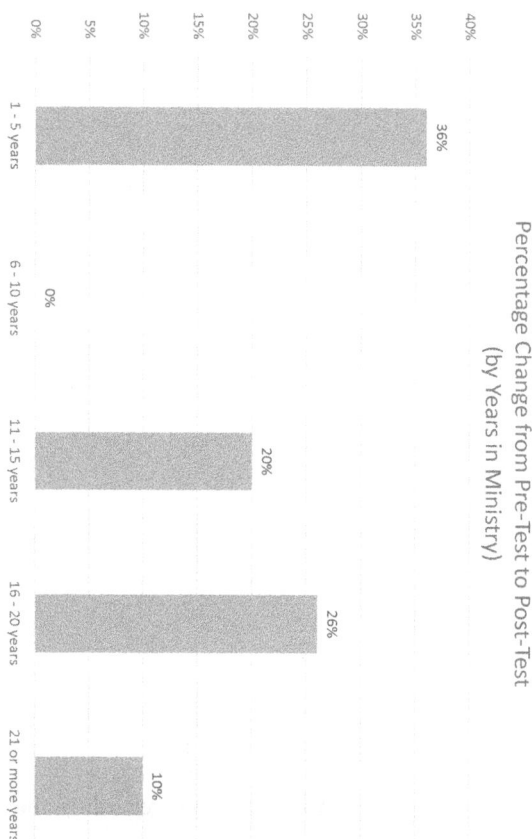

Table J. Percentage Change from Pre-Test to
Post-Test—Years in Ministry

The data indicate that participants who have been in ministry from one to five years showed the most improvement between the Pre-test and Post-test, with a thirty-six percent increase in scores. The next highest improvement scores were the sixteen to twenty years in ministry group.

In the one to five years in ministry group, four of five participants were between forty-one and forty-five years of age. This age group has lived through three major wars and numerous military conflicts.

The data revealed that female participants increased test scores by an average of 40 percent, while male participants increased by an average of 20 percent.

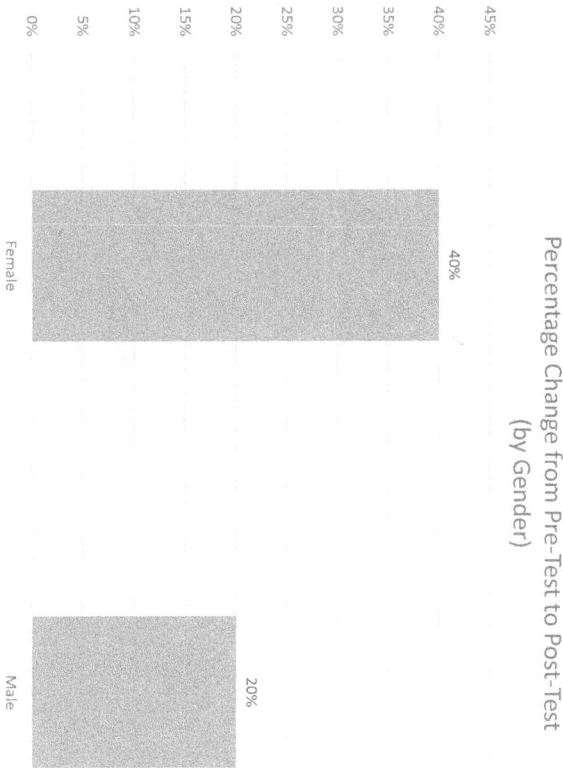

Table K. Percentage Change from Pre-Test to Post-Test—Gender

The forty-six to fifty age range showed the greatest increase between the pre- and post-tests—40 percent. This age band has been exposed to four major wars and numerous military conflicts in their lifetime.

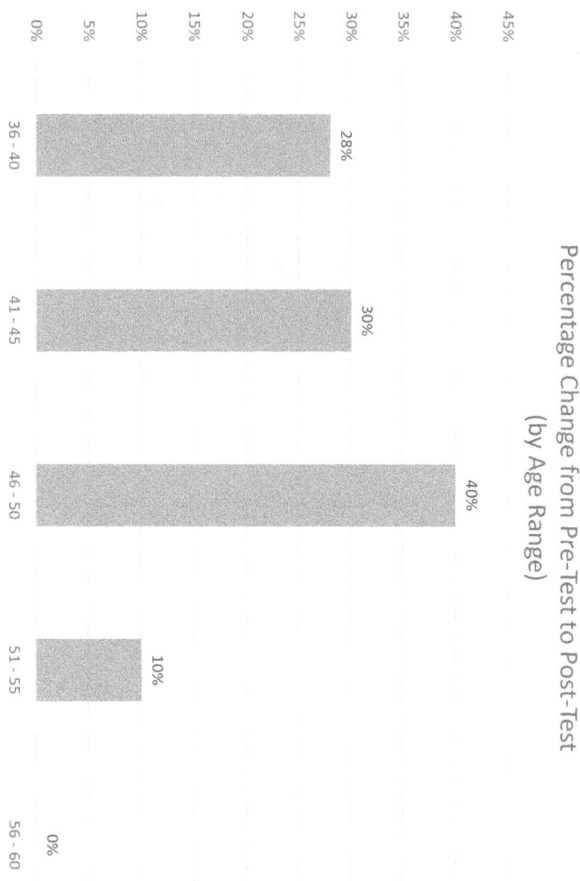

Table L. Percentage Change from Pre-Test
to Post-Test—Age

The Pre-test and Post-test Survey Results

The comparison of the Pre-test and Post-test reflects the outcome of both qualitative and quantitative information. The intent was to capture the participants' assessment of their knowledge of PTSD prior to and after the training. It was also intended to capture the participants' candid comments on the relevance and insights obtained from being a part of the training. The findings are reflected in the following Tables.

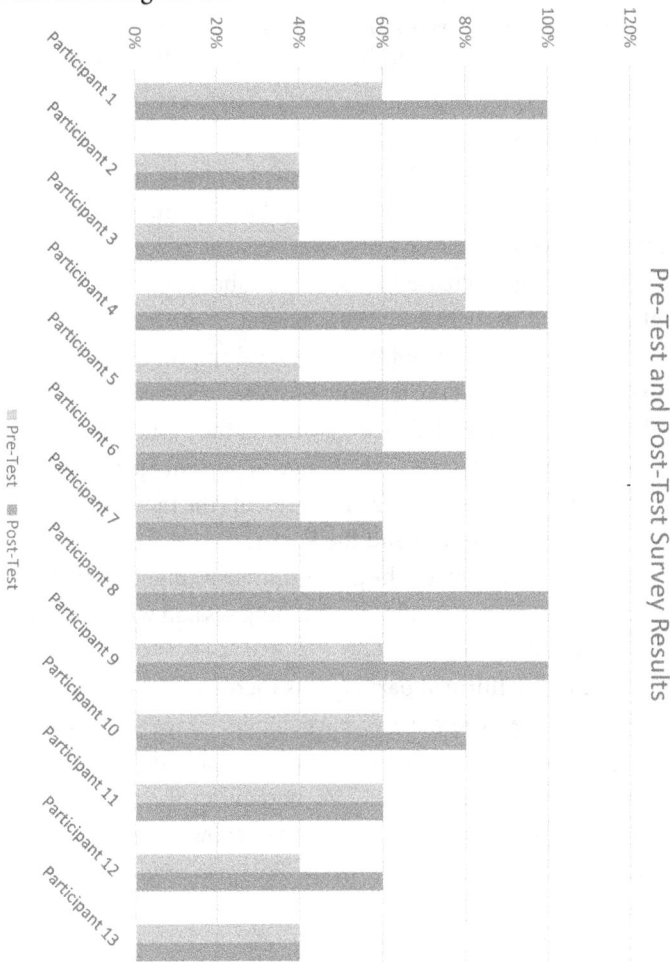

Table M. Pre-Test and Post-Test Survey Results

Table M results are a compilation of both training sessions. It consists of the quantitative portions of the test, Questions 4 through 8. This data represent responses to a total of five questions.

Participant 4 revealed the highest baseline knowledge, scoring 80 percent on the Pre-test administered before the training session. This participant revealed that his/her understanding of PTSD was job related.

Of the remaining twelve participants, five scored 60 percent on the Pre-Test and seven scored 40 percent.

The mean (average) Pre-test score among all the participants was 50 percent; the median score was 40 percent. The mode (occurring the most) for Pre-test scores was 40 percent.

The mean (average) Post-test score among all the participants was 73 percent; the median score was 80 percent. The mode (occurring the most) for Post-test scores was 100 percent.

The average increase in test scores about PTSD was 17 percent among all participants. With ten out of thirteen participants showing at least 20 percent or more level improvement, the data support the belief that the training provided positive improvement in the awareness/knowledge levels among the participants.

Table N demonstrates the change in percentage related to the quantitative portion of the test. It represents the increase in knowledge between the Pre-test and the Post-test.

Participant 8 showed the greatest improvement from the tests administered before and after the training session with an increase of 60 percent in scores.

Four of the thirteen participants increased their scores by 40 percent or more. Another five participants increased their scores by 20 percent or more. Ten of the participants demonstrated an increase in their knowledge. The remaining three participants' knowledge was maintained in that they showed neither increase nor decrease from the Pre-test to the Post-test results.

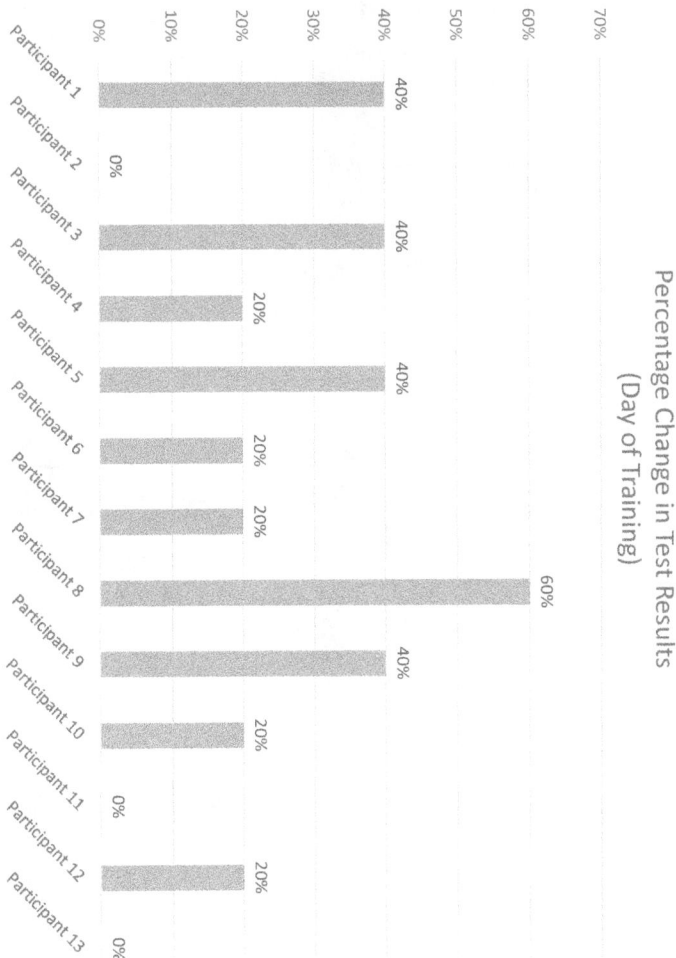

Table N. Test Results (Change in Percentage)
Day of Training

Tables O and P visually depict the additional awareness raised through the classroom experience. This survey question allowed for multiple responses.

As shown in Table O, the participants did not indicate that they had been personally affected by PTSD. Table P shows that as a result of the training session, some participants recognized personal effects of PTSD.

Three of the four categories showed an increase in the Post-test of sources of awareness. The data support, and the tables visually depict, the additional awareness raised through the classroom experience.

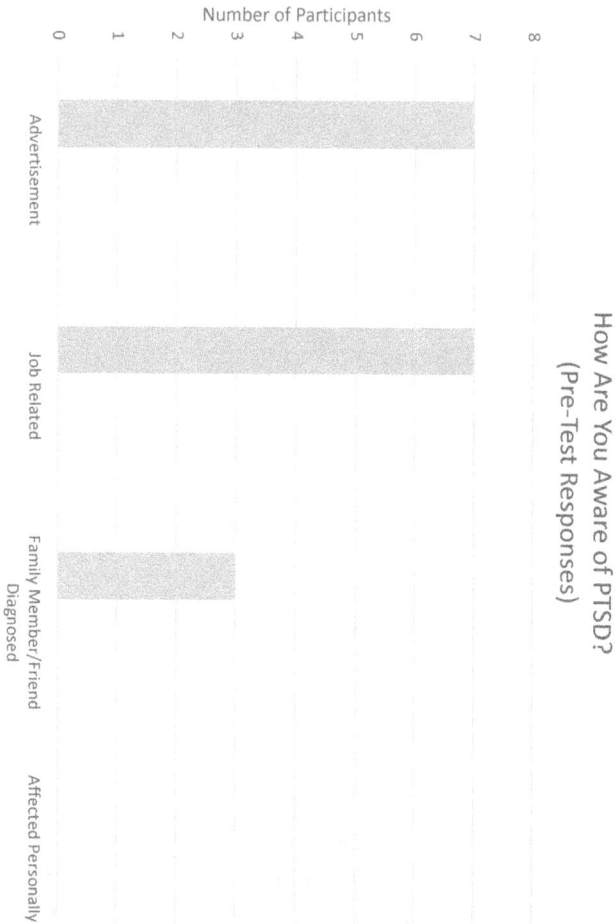

Table O. How Are You Aware of PTSD? (Pre-test)

Number of Participants

How Are You Aware of PTSD?
(Post-Test Responses)

Advertisement

Job Related

Family Member/Friend Diagnosed

Affected Personally

0 1 2 3 4 5 6 7 8 9

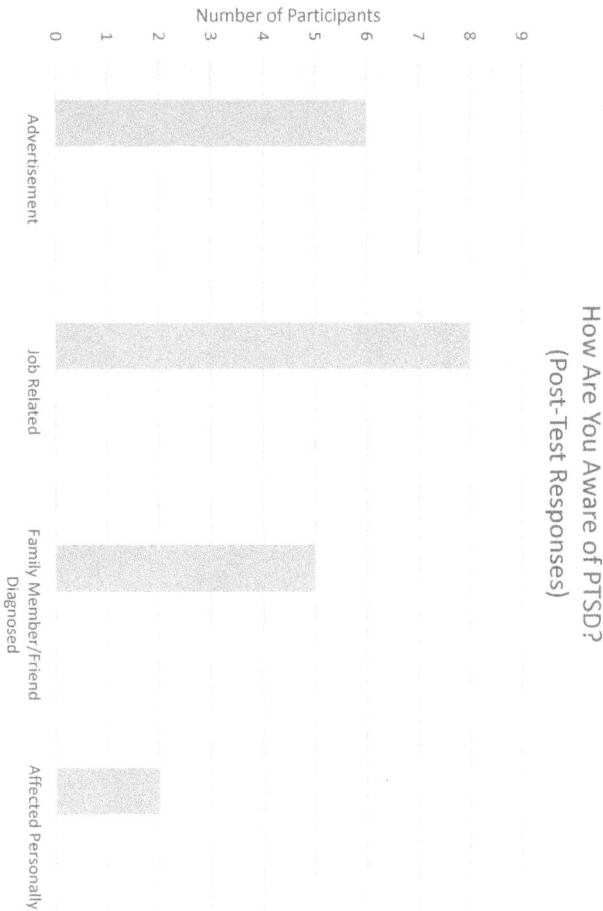

Table P. How Are You Aware of PTSD? (Post-test)

Tables Q and R indicate the effectiveness of the training sessions in raising self-awareness levels related to PTSD.

While six of the thirteen participants indicated minimal awareness of PTSD at the start of the training, no participants indicated this at the end of the training. Six of the participants moved to a higher level of understanding as a result of the training session. Additionally, no participants indicated at the beginning of the training that they were very knowledgeable of PTSD. After the training session, six of the participants felt their awareness had been raised to a higher level.

This data support that the knowledge level was increased by the training provided.

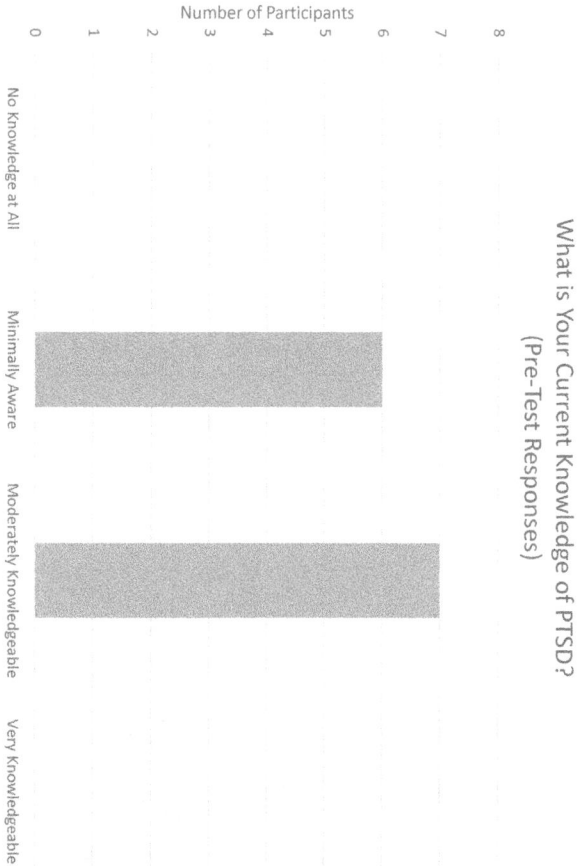

Table Q. What is Your Current Knowledge
of PTSD? (Pre-test)

Number of Participants

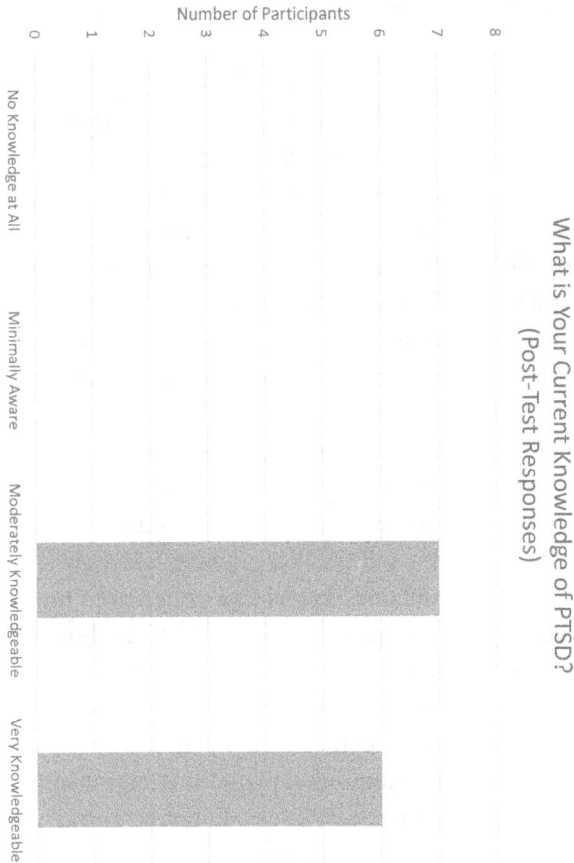

Table R. What is Your Current Knowledge
of PTSD? (Post-test)

The Post-Training Interviews

The post-training interviews consisted of additional qualitative and quantitative data collection, conducted thirty to forty-five days after the initial training. The interviews were intended to measure the sustained knowledge of the participants. Additionally, the post-training interviews provided an opportunity to gauge whether the information provided in the training affected the participants' consciousness and ultimately raised their awareness of PTSD.

Four participants were selected to participate in the post-training interviews. They were selected based on their availability within the specified thirty to forty-five-day timeframe. Each participant was contacted and asked to participate in the one-hour interview. After receiving their consent, meetings were scheduled based on their availability and their preference for location and time. As a result, the post-training interview survey results were collected in an environment different from the initial classroom.

Each interview consisted of two sections. The first section revisited the initial questions from the Post-test given at the conclusion of the training session. These questions were presented in the same paper method as before. Table Q shows that at the post-training interview, one participant showed a 20 percent increase between the Post-test and the Post-training interview test scores. One participant maintained knowledge gained from the Post-test to the post-training interview. Two participants show a 20 percent decrease in test scores; however, neither of these participants dropped below the pre-test scores.

The second portion of the interview consisted of an interview in which qualitative questions explored the impact of the training on the participant's consciousness (awareness) and behaviors. Based on the participant's answers to the qualitative questions, several trends were identified.

Gained New Insights

All the participants' gained new insights and their knowledge of PTSD was increased. Three of the four interviewed attributed their increased awareness specifically to the training by Reverend Mosby. Participant 8 stated, "Understanding PTSD symptoms now helps me understand the struggles my uncle faces." She also shared, "The training made me more sensitive to other types of trauma that keep people from growing relationally."

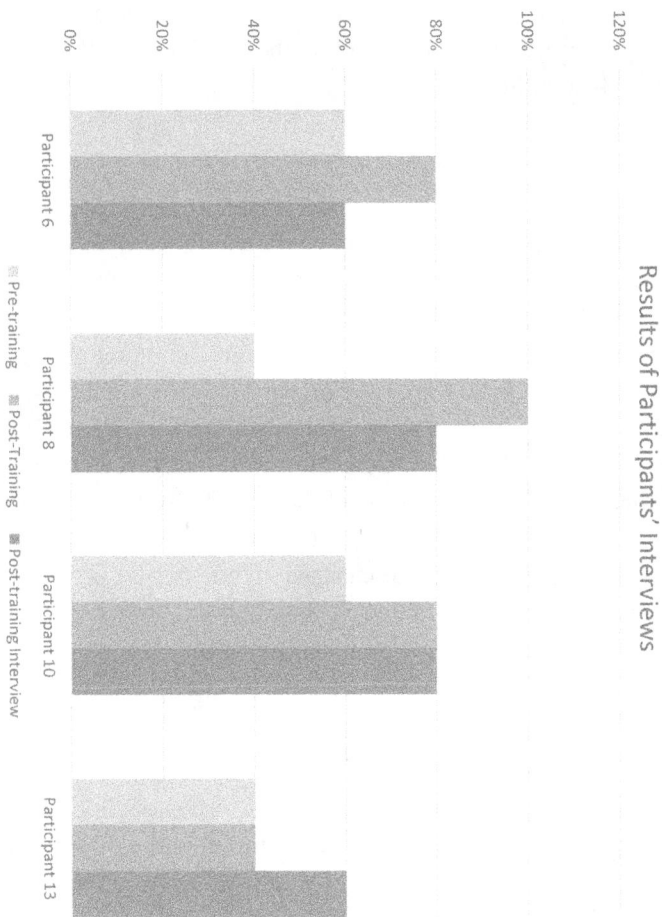

Table S. Participant Interview Results

Impact of Video Presentation

The video helped the participants to understand the military culture and to identify the symptoms of PTSD from someone who suffers from the illness. It also provided a sense of the magnitude of the problem in our society. Participant 8 stated, "The video was beneficial in helping others to understand military culture and their perspective on PTSD." Participant 13 shared, "The film concretized a lot. From the study of the soldier's personal story it opened my eyes to the magnitude of the condition and the need to understand military culture."

Need for Military Ministry

All the participants expressed an affirmative need for military ministries in their churches, elaborating on the benefit the ministry would have on addressing the needs of veterans and their families, while sensitizing the congregation and community to PTSD. Participant 8 commented, "The military ministry would assist in addressing the needs of the veterans and family members. It will also assist in making the congregation more sensitive to the needs of the demographic of the church." Participant 6 stated, "Initially, I would have answered that question with "No." However, since attending the training it has changed my perspective on the need for this ministry in the church. Persons in our churches are in wars and need someone to be an advocate for them."

Shared Knowledge and Information

All the participants shared their increased awareness, information, and resources obtained from the training with others. Participant 8 commented, "Second, I have shared it with other clergy, especially the resources that were given at the session. I feel compelled to help others raise their awareness on this issue." Participant 6 stated, "I have shared freely in Bible study and given freedom to our veterans to talk." He also shared, "I have also shared with other clergy and civic organizations of which I am a part in hopes of peaking community interest and training."

Heightened Personal Awareness

The participants spoke of how their personal awareness was heightened and affected. They shared that their sensitivity to those who are experiencing trauma-related illness has been increased. They also stated that those who are suffering are closer than they realized. Participant 13 stated, "The personal stories from the other pastors in attendance about family members who are suffering made me realize that those who are suffering are closer than I knew." Participant 10 stated, "I am more mindful of stressors and I'm more intentional to keep track of persons that I know are going through stressful situations. If they show symptoms I can now refer them to specific agencies. I am also able to provide them resources." Participant 6 commented, "We, as pastors, need to be more responsive and sensitive. I used to think that only folks with bombs on the battlefield had to deal with this issue. I now know that we have bombs and explosive situations all around us. I serve in the inner city where gun shots in public housing are a constant reality of stress and trauma triggers. We, as pastors, need to be prepared to address peoples' needs and know the resources to refer."

Need for More Training

It was highly recommended by all who were interviewed that others need to be exposed to the reality of the effects of PTSD on our society and participate in this training. Participant 13 commented, "Absolutely. This training should be considered as part of the Christian Education or Pastoral Care course in the Seminary and part of the standard curriculum. Many of the students will pursue pastoral counseling ministry, and there is no current component in their educational track to address and inform them on this subject." He also stated, "The training should be put on DVD so pastors can show it to ministries in their churches. It needs to be documented and distributed." Participant 10 shared, "It is valuable. It really needs to be presented at ministers' meetings or conferences with breakout sessions." Participant 6 commented, "Absolutely. This training is valuable to everyone. It is not just for persons in the military but it is relevant for high crime areas. It would bring heightened awareness to the needs of the community."

Additional Observations

Additional information and observations from the training session can be found in the observers' notes in Appendix K and Appendix L.

Conclusion and Summary

It was the objective of this project to address the void of education and awareness around the issue of Post-Traumatic Stress Disorder in the pastoral community. I see the pastor as a missing resource of interveners who have the responsibility of addressing the spiritual perspective of healing: *soul care*. It was my aspiration to present a context in which pastoral leaders could be introduced to another area of ministry in dire need of their attention and support.

The context offered for this introduction was a workshop. The specific intent of the workshop was to expose the participants to the plight, challenges, and the often-silent voice of those suffering from PTSD. Though the material for the workshop focused strongly on veterans with PTSD, whether military veterans or members of the congregation who have experienced such trauma, there are many who suffer in silence.

This elite group of pastoral leaders was chosen because of the similarity of their call to be spiritual leaders with the charge to provide *soul care* to persons within their congregations and community. It is also the charge of the pastor to bring to the attention of the congregation areas of concern with a need for ministry.

It was my hope that if pastors were enlightened to the need, they would, in turn, empower members of their congregations to be enlightened, educated, and ultimately begin to minister to the needs of their congregation and the veterans in their midst.

Based on the results of this training, I contend that my hypothesis was confirmed. The quantitative data analysis supports my hypothesis that the participants' knowledge of the subject was affected, and in most cases, increased.

The qualitative data support the view that the majority of the participants who attended the workshop validated the need of this training for pastors and others. Further, that view has been confirmed by the number of pastors who are now raising the awareness of others by sharing this subject matter with their congregations through sermons, Bible studies, training, and the development of military ministries within their churches.

Based on the analysis, these are viable steps pastors can take, along with additional training through the Veteran's Administration on PTSD, to further equip and prepare themselves in this area of need.

As I reflect on this work, I believe it would easily be transferrable to other contexts such as Bible studies, conferences, seminars, small group sessions, and the academic classroom. However, it would be difficult for someone who has no prior knowledge or experience with the subject matter of PTSD to be able to effectively present the model as it is currently developed. It would require that the facilitator be trained on the symptomatology of the ailment for the information to be effectively conveyed.

If I had to repeat this project, I would be more accommodating and flexible with time slots for the training. Addressing the time constraints of pastors and their availability, I would consider changing my strategy to promote greater participation, thus, broadening the participation and scope of persons impacted by the materials.

Taking note that both workshops were offered on Saturday mornings, which seemed to be a conflict for most invitees, I would consider offering future workshops during the middle of the day. The consideration of a presentation over an extended lunch timeframe for those with the flexibility to attend midday would be an option. I would offer the training on a weekday evening for bivocational pastors who reserve Saturdays for Sunday preparation and family time.

The lack of participation speaks as loudly to the subject matter as it does for those who participated. Whether the subject matter was of little interest or the timing for the training was not convenient, the lack of participation must be considered for the message it relays. The low participation in this study suggests that one must be cautious in generalizing results of the study to other contexts and populations.

This project was a lived experience. During my research, my interaction with those suffering, and those who have suffered, caused me to examine my own childhood trauma experiences and come face-to-face with my own pain. Coupled with the loss of my brother and grandmother during the course of this project, I was drawn to a closer understanding of the impact trauma can have on a person's life and coping skills. Living through the loss of loved ones during the time I was developing this project, helped me to grow in empathy, healing, and advocacy.

The magnitude of the needs in the veteran's community and in their families is so massive, it was difficult to know where to begin. It was very difficult to narrow the scope of this project. However, as the project unfolded, I began to understand why I was called to address the local pastor as the context for my project. As I watched my son live out this project over six years, it became clear that agents for God (pastors) needed training to assist in the *soul care* of those who suffer.

As Dr. Mark LaRocca-Pitts states, "PTSD is a wound which no amount of pharmacology, behavioral therapy, psychological counseling, or other human intervention can truly heal without the divine intervention of God."[1]

As I prayed for, counseled, and ministered to my son, I witnessed his slow, yet gradual return from the pit of hell to a life full of expectation, hope, and promise because someone cared for his soul. It is this reality that fuels my passion to educate and raise awareness on this subject matter. This reality solidifies my belief that pastors can make a difference in the lives of those whom society would discard.

1. Mark LaRocca-Pitts, "Walking in the Wards of Spiritual Specialist." *Harvard Divinity Bulletin* (2004) www.mirecc.va.gov/docs/visn6/clergyPage. pdf (accessed 9 March 2010).

Appendix A

Survey on Post-Traumatic Stress Disorder

Name (Optional):

Please check one.

Pastor	Assoc. Minister	Chaplain	Min. Chris. Ed.	Other (specify below)

1.	How are you aware of Post-Traumatic Stress Disorder (PTSD)? Check one.
	Affected personally
	Family Member/Friend diagnosed
	Job Related (i.e. Counselor, Chaplain, other)
	Advertisement (TV, News Article, Public Service Announcements)

2.	How do you view the effects of PTSD on your congregation, community, society? Check one.
	State of Emergency—PTSD is a systemic issue that affects everyone.
	Isolated Impact—PTSD is an isolated issue that affects military personnel and their immediate families.
	Minimal Impact—PTSD is a problem but has been contained well by military efforts.
	No Impact—PTSD does not affect our society overall.
	I have not given any thought to the issue one way or another.

3.	Do you know the number of active military in your congregation? Check one.	
	No	
	Yes	Please provide an approximate number.

4.	Do you know the number of veterans in your congregation? Check one.	
	No	
	Yes	Please provide an approximate number.

5.	Is your church within a 30-mile proximity of a military base? Check one.	
	No	
	0-10 miles	
	11-20 miles	
	21-30 miles	

6.	Does your church have an active military ministry/program that addresses PTSD? Check the one that most closely fits your church.		
		Addresses PTSD	Does Not Address PTSD
	We do not have a military ministry.		
	We have an annual program to recognize our military and veteran community within the church.		
	Ministry for our military is a part of another ministry: (please give the name)		
	We have an active military ministry that meets at least quarterly to plan events and offer services.		

7.	Is there interest in developing a comprehensive military ministry/program in your church? Check one.
	There is no interest in development at this time.
	Yes, we have discussed beginning a ministry.
	Yes, we are 1-6 months from implementation.
	Yes, we are 7-12 months from implementation.

8.	Do you provide pastoral counseling for your congregation?	
	Yes	
	No	Go to question 10.

9.	Do PTSD patients require a different education and awareness to provide effective care? Check one.	
	No	
	Yes	Please list any continued learning you have attended.

10.	Would you be interested in more information, training, and tools to be more effective in the clergy care provided to those affected with PTSD?	
	No	
	Yes	Please provide an e-mail address.

~~ Thank you for your time and your participation. Rev. C. Diane Mosby, M.Div. ~~

Appendix B

"When the War Comes Home" Presentation

PTSD involves four main types of symptoms:

- Re-experiencing (repeatedly reliving) the trauma.
  - This can be in the form of nightmares, intrusive memories or images, flashbacks, or intense emotional or physical reactions to reminders of the trauma.
- Physical Hyperarousal
  - This includes sleep problems, anger, irritability, concentration problems, always feeling on edge or on guard, jumpiness, and being easily startled.

Symptoms of PTSD

- Avoidance of trauma reminders.
  - Trying not to think or talk about the trauma, or trying not to have feelings about it.
  - Staying away from activities, people, places and situations that bring up trauma memories.

- Emotional Numbing.
  - Losing interest in activities that used to be important.
  - Feeling detached or estranged from important people in your life.
  - Feeling unable to have normal emotions, and losing a sense of a future for yourself.

Some Facts about PTSD

- PTSD is diagnosed when the symptoms described previously last longer than a month and cause significant distress or impairment in functioning.

- The symptoms of PTSD are often accompanied by other problems, such as depression, hopelessness, drug/alcohol abuse, relationship problems, and physical symptoms (i.e., headaches, stomach upset)

PTSD Facts...

- Symptoms of PTSD many not emerge immediately after the traumatic event. Sometimes it is weeks, months, or even years before the symptoms develop.

- Not all trauma survivors develop PTSD. We do not know all the reasons why some survivors develop it and others do not. But, some of the factors may be genetic, previous experiences with trauma, presence of other stressors, coping skills and social support.

PTSD Facts...

- In the United States, about 8% of the population will have PTSD Symptoms as some point in their lives. Rates are significantly higher among combat veterans.

- PTSD is treatable. There are a number of highly effective interventions available that have been scientifically proven to markedly reduce or even eliminate the symptoms of PTSD.

- This is not a condition persons need to live with forever. Although we cannot change history, but with the right help, we can help change the way that history affects how they live now.

The Wounded Platoon

~ 10 Minute Break ~

When the War Comes Home

- The Military in Our Midst

- Challenges in Returning Home

- Raising Awareness of Pastors and Clergy

- Rebuilding Spirituality and Life

- Pastors and Community Response

The Military In Our Midst

- 1.5 million Service Members have served in Iraq and Afghanistan

- 90% of wounded Service Members survive their injuries

- Over 75% of Service Members surveyed reported having been in situations where they could be seriously injured or killed
  Source: Fact Sheet by Army One Source

The Military in Our Midst...

- More than 62% of them knew someone who was seriously injured or killed

- 38% of Service Members and 31% of Marines report having psychological symptoms
  - PTSD, depression, psychoses, neurotic disorders, and drug and alcohol dependency or abuse

Challenges in Returning Home

- Returning Home is disorienting and can represent a significant change and absence in social community, structure, order, mission, purpose and predictability.

- The enormity of the war experience can shatter the individual's basic sense of safety and the basic understanding of life as they knew it.

Excerpts from "Coming Home" by Dr. John P. Oliver

Challenges in Returning Home...

- In addition, the returning soldier's family are not the same as they were before deployment to war

- Re-adjustment and establishing a "new norm" after the crisis can be complicated and difficult

Challenges in Returning Home...

- Upon returning from war, individuals must "re-set" themselves for civilian life

- Re-setting includes:
  - Grief and transition processing,
  - Un-learning (or re-learning) basic skills such as defensive driving rather than offensive driving
  - Re-developing community support systems

See www.battlemind.org

Raising Awareness of Pastors and Clergy

- Why Pastors and Clergy?

  - Research shows 4 of 10 returning military personnel, veterans and family members will approach their clergy before seeking help from a mental health professional
  - Veterans do not feel comfortable, nor do many of them trust the Veterans Administration and/or other Social Services Agencies
  - Often seeing a member of the clergy is less threatening and has less stigma attached.

Raising Awareness of Pastors and Clergy...

- Spiritual Symptoms of Combat Trauma:

  - Feeling abandoned by God
  - Finding it hard to pray
  - Doubts about core beliefs
  - Anger towards God
  - No Spirit of thankfulness
  - Feelings of alienation of church/friends/family
  - Loss of faith and hope
  - No yearning for righteousness

Spirituality and Rebuilding Life

- Spirituality is that which gives a person meaning and purpose.
    - It is found in relationships with God, Self, Nature and Other ideas.

- Spiritual distress arises when one of these relationships that provide meaning is threatened or broken. The more significant a particular relationship is, the greater the severity of spiritual distress if that relationship is threatened or broken.

- Spiritual wholeness is restored when that which threatens or breaks the patient's relational web of meaning is removed, transformed, integrated, or transcended.

Mark LaRocca-Pitts, Ph.D.

Spirituality and Rebuilding Life...

- Combat trauma on the soldier and his or her family is a deep wound of the soul.

- It is a wound which no amount of pharmacology, behavioral therapy, psychological counseling or other human intervention can truly heal without the divine intervention of God.

Romans 10: 15b,17 (NRSV) shares...

As it is written, **"How beautiful are the feet of those who bring good news!"**

So faith comes from what is heard, and what is heard comes through the word of Christ.

Pastors and Community Response

Who's in the Church?

- If asked, if there are military members/personnel in our church, many church members would respond, "NO" or a "FEW."

- Veterans who have served in past wars, Guardsmen and Reservists who are serving now, and those who have completed whole careers of military service simply do not show up on the churches radar.

- Family Members and Children

Pastors and Community Response...

- A Wounded Soul requires intervention in an environment that churches can provide.
  - Community and relationship (With Christ and Others
  - Pastoral Care (Including counseling and referral)
  - Care and Support (Practical Help/before, during and after deployment)
  - Education (Seminars/Workshops on Marriage Enrichment, Parenting, Finances and other available resources)

Pastors and Community Response...

- "Truly I tell you, just as you did it to one of the least of these who are members of my family, "you did it to me." Mt: 25:40 (NRSV).
- No one system can provide all the services needed
- Supporting the family will support the individual

Pastors and Community Response...

- 78% of survivors receive 100% of their support from family members

- Survivors and caregivers needs are different

Pastors and Community Response...

- We need support groups within our churches (Military Ministry)
  - Groups of volunteers
  - Organized to provide practical, emotional and spiritual support
- The Support System encourages
  - Mutual, respectful relationships
  - Appropriate educational and emotional support

Appendix C

Evaluation Survey

40th Annual Session

American Baptist Churches of the South -- Area II
Riverview Baptist Church, Richmond, VA

EVALUATION SURVEY

Please take a moment to complete the following survey. Check the box that represents your feelings about today's seminar: **Workshop A: When the War Comes Home: Educating Clergy on PTSD.**
Thank you.

	Disagree	Strongly Disagree	Neutral	Agree	Strongly Agree
1. I gained useful knowledge and information.	( )	( )	( )	( )	( )
2. Presentation and handouts were easy to follow and understand.	( )	( )	( )	( )	( )
3. The facilitator was actively involved with participants.	( )	( )	( )	( )	( )
4. The facilitator was knowledgeable and presented ideas and concepts clearly.	( )	( )	( )	( )	( )
5. I believe my time was well spent.	( )	( )	( )	( )	( )
6. I would recommend this seminar to others.	( )	( )	( )	( )	( )
7. Overall, I was very satisfied with the seminar.	( )	( )	( )	( )	( )

8. I would suggest that you make the following improvements to your program: *(Please list below. You may write on back if additional space is needed.)*

_____

_____

_____

Appendix D

Educating Clergy on PTSD

**When the War Comes Home: Educating Clergy on PTSD
Presenter: Reverend C. Diane Mosby**

Number of Attendees Responding

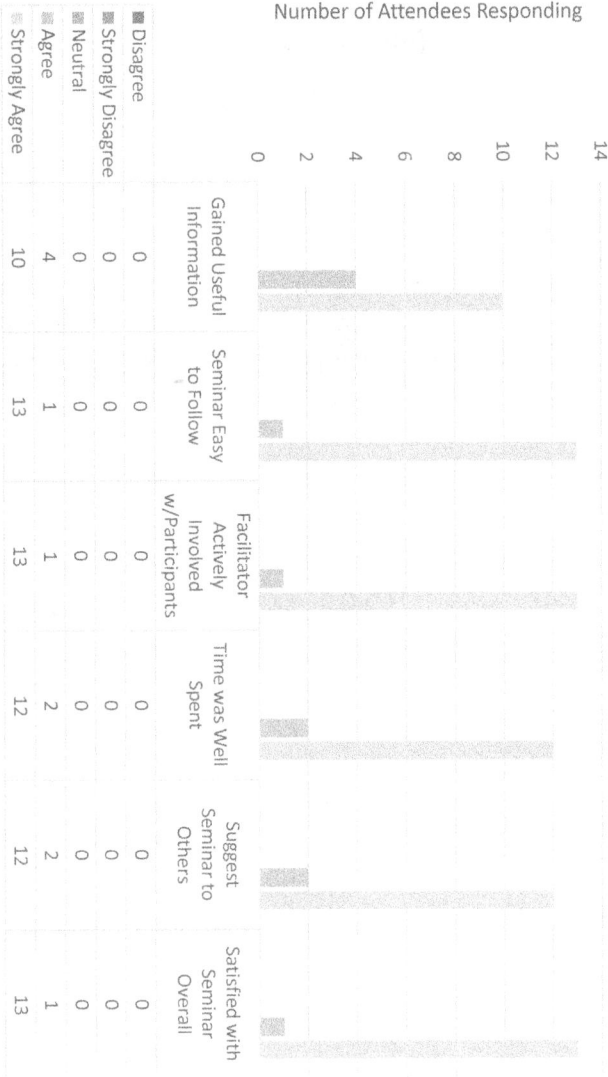

	Gained Useful Information	Seminar Easy to Follow	Facilitator Actively Involved w/Participants	Time was Well Spent	Suggest Seminar to Others	Satisfied with Seminar Overall
Disagree	0	0	0	0	0	0
Strongly Disagree	0	0	0	0	0	0
Neutral	0	0	0	0	0	0
Agree	4	1	1	2	2	1
Strongly Agree	10	13	13	12	12	13

Appendix E

Presentation Feedback

- More time for information. Job well done!
- I am hoping that we can get this info in our church.
- Make this available to others in Churches at large in the local area.
- Excellent!
- Need more seminars at all Annual Sessions.
- This seminar was excellent! The information priceless! Thank you so much for sharing your personal story. May God continue to bless you in your special ministry.

Appendix F

Participant Information Form

Participant Information Form

**When the War Comes Home with Post-Traumatic Stress Disorder (PTSD):
What Pastoral Leaders Need to Know**

I.   **What is your age range?**

☐ 30 – 35   ☐ 36- 40   ☐ 41- 45   ☐ 46- 50   ☐ 51-55   ☐ 56-60
☐ 61 – 65   ☐ 66-70   ☐ 71 – above

II.   **Ethnicity:** _____

III.   **Gender:**   ☐ Male   ☐ Female

IV.   **Marital Status:**   ☐ Married   ☐ Single   ☐ Divorced

V.   **Educational Background: (Check all that apply):**

☐ GED
☐ High School Graduate
☐ Some College
☐ Bachelor's (List Degree)   _____
☐ Master's   (List Degree)   _____
☐ Doctorate (List Degree)   _____
☐ Other   _____

VI.   **Ministry Experience: What capacity are you currently serving?**

☐ Pastor
☐ Associate Pastor
☐ Pastoral Counselor
☐ Christian Education
☐ Other: _____

License (Yr.) _____   Ordained (Yr.) _____   Years serving in ministry: _____

Are you a bi-vocational pastor? ☐ Yes   ☐ No

If yes, what is your other area of employment? (Role/Title)

_____

VII.   **Military Experience: What capacity are you serving or did you serve?**

_____

Years of Service: _____ Branch of Service: _____

Have you ever been diagnosed with Post-Traumatic Stress Disorder? ☐ Yes   ☐ No

Have you ever been treated for Post-Traumatic Stress Disorder?   ☐ Yes   ☐ No

Appendix G

Pre-Test

Pre-Test

When the War Comes Home with Post-Traumatic Stress Disorder (PTSD):
What Pastoral Leaders Need to Know

1. Are you aware of Post-Traumatic Stress Disorder? Yes ☐   No ☐

2. How are you aware of Post-Traumatic Stress Disorder (PTSD)? Check all that apply:
   - ☐ a. Affected personally
   - ☐ b. Job Related (i.e., Counselor, chaplain, other)
   - ☐ c. Family member/Friend diagnosed
   - ☐ d. Advertisement (Television, news article, public service announcement)

3. What is your current knowledge of PTSD?
   - ☐ a. Minimally Aware
   - ☐ b. Moderately Knowledgeable
   - ☐ a. Very Knowledgeable
   - ☐ b. No knowledge at all

4. What is PTSD?
   - ☐ a. A combat related issue
   - ☐ b. An anxiety disorder that can result from exposure to trauma
   - ☐ c. A un-common reaction to an abnormal event
   - ☐ d. All of the above

5. One of the four main symptoms of the ailment is
   - ☐ a. Stigma with the Armed Forces
   - ☐ b. Loss of independence
   - ☐ c. Avoidance of trauma reminders
   - ☐ d. None of the above

6. PTSD has been called the "signature injury" of which war? (Choose all that apply.)
   - ☐ a. Vietnam War
   - ☐ b. Desert Storm
   - ☐ c. OEF (Operation Enduring Freedom- Afghanistan War)
   - ☐ d. OIF (Operation Iraqi Freedom – Iraq War)

7. For every PTSD sufferer from this and past wars, another 10 people are emotionally and spiritually wounded by secondary trauma.
   - ☐ True
   - ☐ False

8. Some of the stigma issues related to veterans and active service members with PTSD are
   - ☐ a. Being seen as weak
   - ☐ b. Unit leaders will treat them differently
   - ☐ c. Harm to their career
   - ☐ d. Lack of trust in the Mental Health Professionals
   - ☐ e. None of the above
   - ☐ f. All of the above

9. Would a military support group (ministry) be helpful in your church?
   - ☐ Yes   ☐ No   If no, why?

Appendix H

Post-Test

Post-Test

When the War Comes Home with Post-Traumatic Stress Disorder (PTSD):
What Pastoral Leaders Need to Know

1. Are you aware of Post-Traumatic Stress Disorder? Yes ☐ No ☐

2. How are you aware of Post-Traumatic Stress Disorder (PTSD)? Check all that apply:
   - ☐ a. Affected personally
   - ☐ b. Job Related
     (i.e., Counselor, chaplain, other)
   - ☐ c. Family member/Friend diagnosed
   - ☐ d. Advertisement (Television, news article, public service announcement)

3. What is your current knowledge of PTSD?
   - ☐ a. Minimally Aware
   - ☐ b. Moderately Knowledgeable
   - ☐ c. Very Knowledgeable
   - ☐ d. No knowledge at all

4. What is PTSD?
   - ☐ a. A combat related issue
   - ☐ b. An anxiety disorder
   - ☐ c. A un-common reaction to an abnormal event
   - ☐ d. All of the above

5. One of the four main symptoms of the ailment is
   - ☐ a. Stigma with the Armed Forces
   - ☐ b. Loss of independence
   - ☐ c. Avoidance of trauma reminders
   - ☐ d. None of the above

6. PTSD has been called the "signature injury" of which war? (Choose all that apply.)
   - ☐ a. Vietnam War
   - ☐ b. Desert Storm
   - ☐ c. OEF (Operation Enduring Freedom- Afghanistan War)
   - ☐ d. OIF (Operation Iraqi Freedom – Iraq War)

7. For every PTSD sufferer from this and past wars, another 10 people are emotionally and spiritually wounded by secondary trauma
   - ☐ True
   - ☐ False

8. Some of the stigma issues related to veterans and active service members with PTSD are
   - ☐ a. Being seen as weak
   - ☐ b. Unit leaders will treat them differently
   - ☐ c. Harm to their career
   - ☐ d. Lack of trust in the Mental Health Professionals
   - ☐ e. None of the above
   - ☐ f. All of the above

9. Would a military support group (ministry) be helpful in your church?
   - ☐ Yes
   - ☐ No   If no, why?

_____

10. Did you gain new insights that increased your knowledge and understanding of PTSD?
    - ☐ Yes
    - No   If yes, what?

_____

Appendix I

Post-Training Interview Questionnaire

Post Interview Questionnaire

When the War Comes Home with Post-Traumatic Stress Disorder (PTSD):
What Pastoral Leaders Need to Know

What do you remember?

1. How are you aware of Post-Traumatic Stress Disorder (PTSD)?

   _____
   _____
   _____
   _____
   _____

2. What is your current knowledge of PTSD?
   - ☐ a. Minimally Aware
   - ☐ b. Moderately Knowledgeable
   - ☐ c. Very Knowledgeable
   - ☐ d. No knowledge at all

3. What is PTSD?
   - ☐ a. A combat related issue
   - ☐ b. An anxiety disorder
   - ☐ c. A un-common reaction to an abnormal event
   - ☐ d. All of the above

4. One of the four main symptoms of the ailment is
   - ☐ a. Stigma with the Armed Forces
   - ☐ b. Loss of independence
   - ☐ c. Avoidance of trauma reminders
   - ☐ d. None of the above

5. PTSD has been called the "signature injury" of which war? (Choose all that apply.)
   - ☐ a. Vietnam War
   - ☐ b. Desert Storm
   - ☐ c. OEF (Operation Enduring Freedom- Afghanistan War)
   - ☐ d. OIF (Operation Iraqi Freedom – Iraq War)

6. For every PTSD sufferer from this and past wars, another 10 people are emotionally and spiritually wounded by secondary trauma
   - ☐ True
   - ☐ False

7. Some of the stigma issues related to veterans and active service members with PTSD are:
   - ☐ a. Being seen as weak
   - ☐ b. Unit leaders will treat them differently
   - ☐ c. Harm to their career
   - ☐ d. Lack of trust in the Mental Health Professionals
   - ☐ e. None of the above
   - ☐ f. All of the above

Reflections and Next Steps:

8. Did you gain new insights that increased your knowledge and understanding of PTSD?

    ☐ Yes   ☐ No   If yes, what?

    _____
    _____
    _____
    _____

9. Would a military support group (ministry) be helpful in your church?

    ☐ Yes   ☐ No   Why/Why not?

    _____
    _____
    _____
    _____

10. Have you shared any of the information/resources gained from the workshop with others?

    ☐ Yes   ☐ No   If yes, who and why?

    _____
    _____
    _____
    _____

11. Did participating in the workshop heighten your awareness of the needs within your congregation?

    ☐ Yes   ☐ No   If yes, how and what did it reveal?

    _____
    _____
    _____
    _____

12. Would you suggest this training to other pastors?

    ☐ Yes   ☐ No   If no, why?

    _____
    _____
    _____
    _____

13. Are there any other comments you would like to share about the workshop, your understanding of PTSD, and what you desire to do with the information you've gained?

    _____
    _____
    _____
    _____

Appendix J

PTSD Presentation

When the War Comes Home with
Post Traumatic-Stress Disorder (PTSD):
What Pastoral Leaders Need to Know.

September 24, 2011

Rev. C. Diane Mosby,
Presenter

Post Traumatic Stress Disorder (PTSD)?

- IS an anxiety disorder that can result from exposure to trauma

- IS a common reaction to an abnormal event

- IS Not limited to the war zone

About PTSD

- PTSD is diagnosed when symptoms of distress last longer than a month and cause impairment in the ability to function

- Symptoms of PTSD many not emerge immediately after the traumatic event

- Not all trauma survivors develop PTSD

Four main types of symptoms:

- Re-experiencing (repeatedly reliving) the trauma

  - Nightmares
  - Intrusive memories or images
  - Flashbacks
  - Intense emotional or physical reactions to reminders of the trauma

- Physical Hyper-arousal

  - Sleep problems
  - Anger
  - Irritability
  - Concentration problems
  - Always feeling on edge or on guard
  - Jumpiness, and being easily startled

- Avoidance of trauma reminders

  - Trying not to think or talk about the trauma
  - Trying not to have feelings about it
  - Staying away from activities, people, places and situations that bring up trauma memories

- Emotional Numbing

  - Losing interest in activities that used to be important.
  - Feeling detached or estranged from important people in your life
  - Feeling unable to have normal emotions, and losing a sense of a future for yourself

PTSD symptoms cont....

- The symptoms of PTSD are often accompanied by other problems, such as:
  - Depression
  - Hopelessness
  - Drug/alcohol abuse
  - Relationship problems
  - Physical symptoms (i.e., headaches, ulcers)

PTSD Facts

- About 8% of the population in the US will have PTSD symptoms at some point in their lives. Rates are significantly higher among combat veterans

- PTSD has been called "the signature injury" of Operation Enduring Freedom (Afghanistan) and Operation Iraqi Freedom (Iraq)

- It is estimated there are over 400,000 Vietnam War Veterans who still suffer from PTSD – undiagnosed and untreated

The Military In Our Midst

~ The Wounded Platoon ~
By PBS/Frontline, 2010

Challenges in Returning Home

• Can be disorienting and can represent a significant change and absence in social community, structure, order, mission, purpose and predictability

• The war experience can shatter the individual's basic sense of safety and understanding of life as they once knew it

Excerpts from "Coming Home" by Dr. John P. Oliver

Challenges in Returning Home...

- Upon returning from war, individuals must "re-set" themselves for civilian life
- Re-setting includes:
  - Grief and transition processing,
  - Un-learning (or re-learning) basic skills such as defensive driving rather than offensive driving
  - Re-developing community support systems

See www.battlemind.org

Challenges in Returning Home...

- For every PTSD sufferer from this and past wars, another 10 people are emotionally and spiritually wounded by the secondary trauma created by the sufferer's behavior

Spiritual Issues

- A "Crisis of Faith" is a condition in which a person's normal, established relationship with God, or one's spiritual worldviews are violated and appear helpless or useless.

- This is crisis of faith is a "soul care issue."

- Deep physical, psychological, and spiritual wounds are all war related issues that threaten the mind, body and soul, causing a number of physical, emotional, mental and spiritual challenges

Spiritual Symptoms

- Many survivors speak of feeling dead inside, as if, their essence was destroyed
  - The war stole my sole
  - I died spiritually
  - I feel dead inside

- Oftentimes this type of conversation speaks about a <u>death of meaning</u> and <u>purpose</u>, and <u>the loss of connection with God</u>

Spiritual Symptoms of Combat Trauma

- Feeling abandoned by God
- Finding it hard to pray
- Doubts about core beliefs
- Anger towards God
- No Spirit of thankfulness
- Feelings of alienation of church/friends/family
- Loss of faith and hope
- No yearning for righteousness
- Seeing no value in scripture

Why the need for Pastors and Clergy?

- Research shows 4 of 10 returning military personnel, veterans and family members will approach their clergy before seeking help from a mental health professional

- Many veterans do not feel comfortable, nor do many of them trust the Veterans Administration and/or other Social Services Agencies

- Often seeing a member of the clergy is less threatening and has less stigma attached.

- Some of the stigma issues are:
  - Seen as weak
  - Unit leaders will treat them differently
  - Unit will have less confidence in you
  - Harm to their career
  - Embarrassing
  - Lack of trust in the Mental Health Professionals

Pastors and clergy...

- Combat trauma on the soldier and his or her family is a deep wound of the soul

- It is a wound which no amount of pharmacology, behavioral therapy, psychological counseling or other human intervention can truly heal without the divine intervention of God

Ezekiel 37: 1- 3a shares...

"The hand of the Lord came upon me, and he brought me out by the Spirit of the Lord and set me down in the middle of the valley; it was full of bones.

He led me all around them; there were many lying in the valley, and they were very dry. He said to me, "Mortal man, can these bones live?" (NRSV)

Pastors ...

- PTSD is a crisis. During a time of crisis many will call on their pastor first.

- The response to this crisis from pastors who serve as educators and leaders can assist in the outcome on whether these dry bones will live again.

- Pastors who function as agents for God, this crisis is a call to help usher persons from desperation, hopelessness and a lifeless state of existence to restoration and healing

- No one system can provide all the services needed

- A Wounded Soul requires intervention in an environment where pastors are:

  – Keenly aware
  – Educated
  – And leading churches to respond by providing support

Pastors and Community Response

  – Pastoral Care (Including counseling and referral)

  – Community and relationship (With Christ and Others)

  – Care and Support (Practical Help/before, during and after deployment)

  – Education (Seminars/Workshops on Marriage Enrichment, Parenting, Finances and other available resources)

Pastors...

With your help we can make a difference in the lives we serve. Healing and restoration is possible.

Thank You!!!

Appendix K

The Observer's Documentation A

Reverend Cholon Coleman served as the observer for the first training session held on September 24, 2011. As outlined in Section 3 of Chapter 4, her role was to assist in the administrative needs for the training and to audit the proceedings of the training class. The documentation from her observation is noted herein.

Prior to session's beginning: 10 people are expected to attend; room temperature is comfortable.

9:09 a.m.   Session began. Facilitator thanked participants for attending (seven present).

9:12 a.m.   Consent form was explained. Note: Participants intentionally were reading consent form.

9:14 a.m.   Green sheet – demographic info for research explained. Note: Participants appeared not to mind completing form. A female participant had one question about the information on the demographic sheet that was addressed by Reverend Mosby.

9:16 a.m.   It was asked if there were any veterans as participants. There was one. Reverend Mosby thanked him for his service. Two additional persons arrived late and were asked to fill out the IRB consent form and the Pre-Test Survey Form.

9:18 a.m.   Session began. Participants were actively listening.

Pre-Survey Form about knowledge base – participants were not rushing and seemed thorough in reading and answering the questions on the form.

9:26 a.m.   *Question:* A participant asked about the relevance of the information to the community and congregations.

Reverend Mosby gave an explanation of how and why this topic was chosen for her dissertation. In definition she explained how the participant's question is relevant to the community and congregation.

Note: Participants are in thinking posture. There is verbal acknowledgement of information provided. Reverend Mosby offered a good explanation of trauma triggers.

Question: Participant asked about additional clarity on Reverend Mosby's son and how the family addressed his trauma triggers.

Reverend Mosby shared a personal experience that happened around a family cookout that addressed the participant's question.

9:35 a.m.   *Note:* Participants actively engaged and listened to examples of everyday life and traumatic events. Good statistics are given.

Question: Participant raised a question about the statistics of the staggering number of homeless veterans and the concern that most are in denial about the disorder.

Reverend Mosby addressed the statistics through her research and her personal knowledge through her work and association with the Division of Homeless Veterans at McGuire Veterans Affairs Medical Center.

Note: Reverend Mosby's use of identifying the participants by name drew them into the conversation. The participant's response was to sit up straighter and become more active in his listening posture.

Question: Are there resources available to help from the military?

Reverend Mosby responded to the question by sharing that initially the VA was not prepared for the magnitude of soldiers returning from war who were and are suffering with PTSD. Since 2004 there has been an increased recognition of the need for additional programs within and outside of the VA to address the problem. Some of the programs are now available through the United States Department of Veterans Affairs and the VET Centers in most cities. She also shared about the Veterans of Foreign Wars Organizations (VFW), and many grass roots centers and organizations that are now being developed and offering assistance.

Question: What have we learned from the Vietnam War?

Reverend Mosby responded that we have learned that war has casualties of wounded soldiers and veterans. Some of those affected carry the invisible wounds of war. Even though we learned that Vietnam Veterans were affected mentally from the war, the Veterans Administration was still not prepared for the numbers of returning veterans affected from the Afghanistan and Iraq Wars.

9:55 a.m.   The video was introduced and told it would last ten minutes. Participants were informed about the possible disturbing nature of some of the video and were encouraged to step out if necessary.

10:06 a.m.   Participants were asked if they wanted a break: participants did not and the session continued.

10:08 a.m.   Questions/Observations of video

- Observation of the statement made by the platoon commander helped participants to better understand the military culture

- Observation that benefits are not eligible for persons who have a general discharge from the military

- Observation of the psychological injury of the soldier in the film – denial of the soldier issues by his commander

- Observation of the differences of soldiers with physical injuries and those with PTSD and the disparity of benefits
- Observation of the struggle with stigmas in the military and why some will not come forward to receive help
- There was continued good discussion about preparing soldiers returning home.
- One of the participants who is a Vietnam Veteran compared the Vietnam War with Desert Storm, Iraq, and Afghanistan Wars and noted some of the similar challenges of the veterans after the war.
- Great discussion on socio-economic, legislative, and social issues as it pertains to veterans, PTSD, and benefits

10:19 a.m.   Returning Home section of the presentation is discussed.

Note: Participants appear to be actively engaged and showing no signs of boredom or fatigue.

Note: to the facilitator – when giving personal examples, slow the facilitator's speech down. She began to rush just a tad bit.

10:26 a.m.   Spiritual Issues discussed

Observation: A conversation ensued about the issues of weapons and the Word conflict. How do persons reconcile what you have to do to survive by the weapon vs. what you have been taught and know through the Word of God?

Comment: The Vietnam Veteran stated that the military is not concerned with faith issues. "You are trained to do a job, period." The participant made comment that this is an ongoing challenge.

Question from another pastor: "What is the involvement of the church with veterans or those struggling with PTSD?"

Comment: Another pastor spoke to the issue of stigmas in the military and the lack of trust of veterans with the VA. He stated we (clergy) must take an active part and make mental health referrals; most tend to shut down at the mention of referral; this takes time and is an investment to soul care.

The question was then broached, "Do we (clergy) believe in restoration?

After several minutes of dialogue, Reverend Mosby shared that this is the reason for this project and for this discussion. There is a need to bring forth a platform where persons can be trained, their awareness raised, and to be able to ask and wrestle with role of pastors to their congregations and the veterans in various congregations and community. She continued by sharing that soul care is a calling each pastor has been charged with and if pastors do not believe in or are willing to promote that restoration is possible then, when and, from whom will those who are suffering find hope and hear that healing and restoration is possible?

10:45 a.m.   Pastors and Community – How can we help?

Note: All participants are really engaged and actively listening.

- Good laughing moments helped to lighten the mood of the heaviness of the topic.

- Good talking moments using examples to show how lengthy the process is: finances, getting benefits, support, assistance, tolerance, acceptance, need for more training and a broader base for this type of training.

10:56 a.m.   Closing Statements

Question: Participant raised the concern: "What things have been done for your congregation?"

Reverend Mosby shared some of the things that have been done at Anointed New Life Baptist Church, such as: Bible studies around the topic, Prayer Vigil, dedication of the Prayer Wall to remember those who have served and given the ultimate sacrifice, their life, worship service focused for Veterans and Active Duty Service persons to include bringing the Vet Mobile Center on site to provide resources, assistance, and referral to those in the congregation and community, identifying veterans in the congregation and personally thanking them for their service and inviting them to assist in Military Ministry. She shared there are so many ways to raise awareness in congregations and in the communities they serve and offered her assistance to help them get started.

Observation: Another participant shared what impact this presentation could have if it was done at STVU in Christian Education or Pastoral Care to equip our student/clergy on such issues as this.

Observation: This presentation needs to be expanded to include persons who are returning to society from incarceration. It would be very helpful to prison ministry.

Comment: Knowing the right connections makes a world of difference.

11:05 a.m.   Post Survey – Participants were asked to complete the survey.

11:10 a.m.   Additional Resources were shared with the participants and given to them to take with them at the conclusion of the session.

Comment: Participants wanted to know what happened to Nash (soldier in the movie). *Reverend Mosby shared his outcome in the documentary and shared that his story is not as isolated as persons want to believe.*

11:27 a.m.   Another participant commented on Michelle Obama's platform for the military and PTSD.

Note: Participants are still actively engaged. They offer good questions and seem to want social change. They are able to identify with this topic very well. Each time the facilitator tried to close, another question or statement would start another discussion.

Comment: Participant asked Reverend Mosby that the next time she does the presentation to please expand the clip in the documentary of the commander's disregard of the soldiers cry for help. He stated it was a pungent point and an eye opener about military culture.

11:34 a.m.   Reverend Mosby concludes the class and offers the participants refreshments and additional time to continue their conversations.

Appendix L

The Observer's Documentation B

Mrs. Carol Watkins served as the observer for the first training session held on December 3, 2011. As outlined in Section 3 of Chapter 4, her role was to assist in the administrative needs for the training and to audit the proceedings of the training class. The documentation from her observation is noted herein.

There were seven pastors confirmed to attend the session, *When the War Comes Home with Post-Traumatic Stress Disorder: What Pastoral Leaders Need to Know*, a workshop explaining the effects of Post-Traumatic Stress Disorder (PTSD). It is currently 9:03 a.m., and two ministers are present for the training.

Notes: The facilitator has provided refreshments for the invitees. The smaller conference room has been prepared for light refreshments and coffee. The larger conference room is set to accommodate seven ministers. The table contains all materials for the presentation. The PowerPoint presentation is displayed on the screen awaiting start. The facilitator is doing a good job of making small talk as we wait to start.

While waiting, the facilitator led the invitees to complete consent forms for IRB, participant information, and the Pre-Survey form. It appears that the facilitator and the attendees have a good relationship, and the comfort level seems high.

We now have three participants. The facilitator began by sharing the agenda of the day and for her calling to train on PTSD. Introductions were made so that all could continue the comfort level. Presently, participants look engaged. The disclaimer that material may be sensitive was given. Participants completed the pre-survey.

Cover slide of the PowerPoint presentation reflects a wall of honor with the American flag showing. Flowers are also shown as a memorial to the fallen.

The facilitator began to stress the reason for this particular workshop and gave a definition of PTSD. As she moved into the topic, she presented a picture of how PTSD can affect others, such as rape victims, victims of domestic violence, natural disaster, and tragic events like 9/11. One of the participants offered that it could also be caused by an unexpected death of a loved one.

Another invitee arrives and there are now four in attendance. In an effort to bring the new arrival up to speed, and at the risk of losing the interest of others who had already been given the information, the facilitator requested of the participants a few minutes to allow the attendee the opportunity to complete the IRB consent form and the pre-test survey.

Attention of the participants remained high as evidenced by good eye contact and the acknowledgement of interest with nodding of heads, grunts, and verbal agreement.

Question: A participant asked the facilitator to speak on the relationship problems experienced by victims. That question seemed to pique the interest of all.

Again, all eyes were on Reverend Mosby as she discussed the statistics on the high rate of divorce, domestic violence, and substance abuse among those suffering with PTSD.

Question: "How do you help victims who do not want to talk about the experience?"

Reverend Mosby addressed the question by sharing that prayer, patience, and allowing persons to know that they have a safe space with persons they can trust is important. One of the most difficult issues about persons with PTSD is denial, and it requires persons who have the proper training to be able to make progress with them. However, we should all be sensitive to the fact that we should not try to force sufferers to talk about experiences that they do not want to relive.

Question: "How do you deal with numbing?"

Reverend Mosby did an excellent job of deferring the question to later in the presentation, but she gave a bit of reasoning as to why some persons result to numbing as a coping mechanism to stressors.

Another minister shared an experience of a person in her congregation who needed help. A good discussion ensued!

Another pastor recalled an experience of an accident and how he had symptoms of PTSD but was able to recover.

Reverend Mosby explained that one can have symptoms of PTSD but not have the "illness" unless the symptoms are prolonged and cause impairment with daily living, coping, and abilities.

The video clip was shown. It is now 10:32 a.m., and beyond the break. Caution...

Question: "How did you know your son was not crazy?"

Reverend Mosby shared her story. She stated she knew her son. The six-year journey that the pastor endured with the affairs of her son struck visible emotion with the attendees and sparked a lot of conversation.

Note: Correct the word "sole" to "soul" on the presentation.

Participants started a stream of conversation regarding how they themselves can deal with blacks and the military. How they can intervene as a group. What they can do to help protect. They began to dissect the problem, became eager, and charged to solve the issue, and how to help find a solution to the problem.

In summary, the Ezekiel dry bones Scripture was read. A word to the pastors was given regarding how they should respond to the issues of soul care. Many tips and suggestions were provided to them in order to create safe spaces.

For their further interest, the facilitator explained the information that was on display. Many questions were asked from the group about resources and referral information.

Glossary

Deployment.
The positioning of military forces into a formation for battle.

Dishonorable Discharge (DD).
A punitive discharge from military service due to issues of reprehensible conduct or performance.

Etiology.
The study of causes or origins.

General Discharge.
A discharge from military service of a person who has served honorably but who has not met all the conditions of an honorable discharge.

Global War on Terrorism (GWOT).
The War on Terror (also known as the Global War on Terror or the War on Terrorism) is a term commonly applied to an international military campaign led by the United States and the United Kingdom with the support of other NATO as well as non-NATO countries.

Honorable Discharge.
Discharged from military service with a commendable record.

Improvised Explosive Device (IED).
A device placed or fabricated in an improvised manner incorporating destructive, lethal, noxious, pyrotechnic, or incendiary chemicals that are designed to destroy, or incapacitate.

Other Than Honorable Discharge (OTH).
An administrative discharge from military service due to issues of unacceptable conduct or performance.

Post-Traumatic Stress Disorder (PTSD).
An anxiety disorder that can result from exposure to trauma.

Soul Care.
> The act of providing assistance with the facilitation of healing and spiritual wellness through a restored connection of core beliefs and a reconciled personal relationship with God.

Symptomatology.
> The combined symptoms of a disease.

Theater Veteran.
> A military service member who has served in a combat zone of the Armed Forces.

Veteran.
> A military service member who has served in the Armed Forces.

Bibliography

Anderson, Robert C. *The Effective Pastor: A Practical Guide to the Ministry.* Chicago: Moody, 1985.

Cantrell, Bridget C., and Chuck Dean. Down Range to Iraq and Back. Washington: WordSmith, 2005.

Cooper-Lewter, Nicholas and Henry H. Mitchell. Soul Theology: The Heart of American Black Culture. Nashville: Abingdon, 1991.

Day, Jackson, et. al. Risking Connection in Faith Communities: A Training Curriculum for Faith Leaders Supporting Trauma Survivors. Maryland: Sidran Institute, 2006.

Goulston, Mark. Post-Traumatic Stress Disorder for Dummies. New Jersey: Wiley, 2008.

Hatcher, Edgar W. "Care for Returning Veterans Workshop." Lutheran Theological Southern Seminary//News. September 10, 2008. Accessed October 23, 2010. http://www.ltss.edu/news/latest-news/32/.

Hoge, Charles W.,et al. "Combat Duty in Iraq and Afghanistan, Mental Health Problems, and Barriers to Care." New England Journal of Medicine 351 (July 1, 2004).

Imhoff, Frank. "Congregations Prepare Care for Veterans Returning from War." The Lutheran. September 4, 2008. Accessed November 9, 2010. http://www.thelutheran.org/blog/index.cfm?person_id=296. Frontline, WGBH Educational Foundation. The Wounded Platoon. 2010.

Kulka , Richard A. et al. "Trauma and the Vietnam War Generation: Report of Findings from the National Vietnam Veterans Readjustment Study." New York: Brunner/Mazel, 1990.

LaRocca-Pitts, Mark. "Walking in the Wards of Spiritual Specialist." Harvard Divinity Bulletin. 2004. Accessed March 9, 2010. http://www.mirecc.va.gov/docs/visn6/clergyPage.pdf.

Lewis, Phillip V., "Transformational Leadership: A New Model for Total Church Involvement." (Broadman and Holman: Nashville), 1996,14.

Meagher, Ilona. Moving a Nation to Care: Post-Traumatic Stress Disorder and America's Returning Troops. New York: IG, 2007.

Ministering to the Military: A Guide for Churches. Newport News: Military Ministry, 2009.

"Obama: U.S. on Track in Afghanistan, Pakistan—Army News|News from Afghanistan & Iraq - Army Times." Army Times. December 16, 2010. Accessed January 15, 2011. http://www.armytimes.com/news/2010/12/ap-obama-says-us-on-track-in-afghanistan-pakistan-121610/.

Proctor, Samuel. My Moral Odyssey. Pennsylvania: Judson, 1989.

"PTSD and Community Violence: A National Fact Sheet." Research and Education on Post-Traumatic Stress Disorder. Accessed October 10, 2010. http://ptsdinfo.org/#ncptsd

Ramsay, Nancy J., Pastoral Diagnosis: A Resource for Ministers of Care and Counseling. Minneapolis: Fortress, 1998.

"Record Number of Army Suicides in June." Screening for Mental Health. August 12, 2010. Accessed September 9, 2010. http://www.mentalhealthscreening.org/enews/sosanni.aspx.

Rosenbloom, Dena, et al. Life After Trauma, Second Edition. New York: Guilford, 2010.

Schiraldi, Glen R. The Post-Traumatic Stress Disorder Sourcebook, Second Edition: A Guide to Healing, Recover, and Growth. New York: McGraw, 2009.

Sigmund, Judith A., "Spirituality and Trauma: The Role of Clergy in the Treatment of Posttraumatic Stress Disorder." Journal of Religion and Health (Volume 42, Number 3) 221–229.

Sippola John, et al. Welcome Them Home: Help Them Heal: Pastoral Care and Ministry with Service Members Returning from War. Minnesota: Whole Person Associates, 2009.

"Spirituality and Trauma: Professionals Working Together."—NATIONAL CENTER for PTSD. April 11, 2011. Accessed July 12, 2011. http://www.ptsd.va.gov/professional/pages/fs-spirituality.asp.

Tanielian Terri, and L. H. Jaycox, eds. "Invisible Wounds of War: Psychological and Cognitive Injuries. Their Consequences, and Services to Assist Recovery." RAND. 2008. Accessed July 12, 2011. http://www.rand.org/multi/military/veterans.html

Tick, Edward. War and Soul: Healing Our Nation's Veterans from Post-Traumatic Stress Disorder. Illinois: Theosophical, 2005.

Weaver, Andrew J., et al. "Posttraumatic Stress, Mental Health Professionals and the Clergy: A Need for Collaboration, Training and Research." Journal of Traumatic Stress (Volume 9, Number 4) 847–856.

Weaver, A.J.,et al. (1997). What Do Psychologists Know About Working with the Clergy? An Analysis of Eight APA Journals: 1991–1994. Professional Psychology—Research & Practice, 28 (5), 471–474.

Weaver, Andrew J., "Psychological trauma: What clergy need to know." Journal of Pastoral Psychology (Volume 41, Number 6) 385–408.

Wright H. Norman, Crisis Counseling: A Practical Guide for Pastors, Counselors and Friends (Regal: Ventura), 1993, 10.